Cambridge Elements ≡

Elements in Contemporary Performance Texts
edited by
Fintan Walsh
Birkbeck, University of London
Duška Radosavljević
Royal Central School of Speech and Drama, University of London
Caridad Svich
Rutgers University

THEATRICALITY, PLAYTEXTS AND SOCIETY

David Barnett
University of York

W0010055

CAMBRIDGE
UNIVERSITY PRESS

CAMBRIDGE
UNIVERSITY PRESS

Shaftesbury Road, Cambridge CB2 8EA, United Kingdom

One Liberty Plaza, 20th Floor, New York, NY 10006, USA

477 Williamstown Road, Port Melbourne, VIC 3207, Australia

314–321, 3rd Floor, Plot 3, Splendor Forum, Jasola District Centre, New Delhi – 110025, India

103 Penang Road, #05–06/07, Visioncrest Commercial, Singapore 238467

Cambridge University Press is part of Cambridge University Press & Assessment, a department of the University of Cambridge.

We share the University's mission to contribute to society through the pursuit of education, learning and research at the highest international levels of excellence.

www.cambridge.org
Information on this title: www.cambridge.org/9781009506298

DOI: 10.1017/9781009506311

© David Barnett 2024

This publication is in copyright. Subject to statutory exception and to the provisions of relevant collective licensing agreements, with the exception of the Creative Commons version the link for which is provided below, no reproduction of any part may take place without the written permission of Cambridge University Press & Assessment.

An online version of this work is published at doi.org/10.1017/9781009506311 under a Creative Commons Open Access license CC-BY-NC 4.0 which permits re-use, distribution and reproduction in any medium for non-commercial purposes providing appropriate credit to the original work is given and any changes made are indicated. To view a copy of this license visit https://creativecommons.org/licenses/by-nc/4.0

When citing this work, please include a reference to the DOI 10.1017/9781009506311

First published 2024

A catalogue record for this publication is available from the British Library.

ISBN 978-1-009-50629-8 Hardback
ISBN 978-1-009-50628-1 Paperback
ISSN 2753-2798 (online)
ISSN 2753-278X (print)

Cambridge University Press & Assessment has no responsibility for the persistence or accuracy of URLs for external or third-party internet websites referred to in this publication and does not guarantee that any content on such websites is, or will remain, accurate or appropriate.

Theatricality, Playtexts and Society

Elements in Contemporary Performance Texts

DOI: 10.1017/9781009506311
First published online: May 2024

David Barnett
University of York
Author for correspondence: David Barnett, david.barnett@york.ac.uk

Abstract: This Element proposes a novel way of defining, understanding and approaching theatricality, a term that exists both in the theatre and, more broadly, in everyday life. It argues that four foundational, material processes of theatre-making manifest themselves in all playtexts in both overt and covert forms. Each of the four sections defines a different theatrical process, explores its functions in two chosen playtexts and examines its implications for the wider experience of the spectators outside the theatre. The Element concludes with a supplementary reflection on performance to show how even seemingly untheatrical playtexts can be analysed and staged to reveal their unspoken theatricality. It also argues that this new understanding of theatricality has a politics, that the artifice of any theatre and the constructedness of any society are analogous and that both, consequently, can be fundamentally changed. This Element is also available as Open Access on Cambridge Core.

Keywords: theatricality, theatre and everyday life, theatre and politics, metatheatre, play analysis

© David Barnett 2024

ISBNs: 9781009506298 (HB), 9781009506281 (PB), 9781009506311 (OC)
ISSNs: 2753-2798 (online), 2753-278X (print)

Contents

An Introduction to Theatricality

A new study of theatricality would perhaps not be necessary if scholars could agree on what the term means and what it might imply. However, as the two opening sections of this Introduction will show, scholars have grappled long and hard with these issues, and I will consider a number of definitions and understandings while also drawing attention to their limitations. In the final section, I will propose my own approach to how one might conceptualize and investigate theatricality.

In the rest of the Element, I will examine nine different playtexts for how they articulate theatricality. These examples may encourage readers to adopt the approaches I have taken and apply them to their own choices in order to discover what an analysis of a playtext's theatricality can reveal about its relationship to itself and to the world beyond the stage. As will become evident, theatricality is often closely associated with performance rather than the plays that give rise to it. However, as the subsequent sections will show, investigating a playtext will help reveal how it negotiates the various facets I define as contributing to its theatricality. With this in mind, I will not be discussing live art in order to ground my ideas in a method best applied to the written word, but which can nonetheless extend beyond it.

And rather than talking about plays, I deliberately use the term 'playtext'. This has two advantages. First, playtext clearly prioritizes the words on the page, how they can identify theatricality, and thus provide a starting point to fathoming its implications. Second, playtext moves beyond an understanding of plays as drama. So, while many playtexts can be considered dramas, more recent examples exhibit qualities associated with postdramatic theatre.[1] The method outlined at the end of this Introduction applies to playtexts as a whole, and indeed, readers will find some postdramatic elements in the plays I have chosen for investigation.

My focus on playtexts, however, does not suggest a return to logocentrism, the belief that, in this case, the printed words hold an ultimate truth as to a play's meaning as a representation of reality. Richard Sheppard offers a useful problematization of this position:

> The signified of any text is not a unifying idea, principle, energy or repertoire, but a meta-textual dialectic out of which that text has been generated and which consists, simultaneously, in a set of problems and a set of responses.[2]

---

[1] This is not the place to consider the differences between dramatic and postdramatic playtexts, but interested readers may consult my 'When is a Play not a Drama? Two Examples of Postdramatic Theatre Texts', *New Theatre Quarterly*, 24: 1 (2008), pp. 14–23 for a more detailed discussion.

[2] Richard Sheppard, *Tankred Dorst's 'Toller': A Case Study in Reception* (New Alyth: Lochee, 1989), p. 9.

That is, meaning *only* emerges from complex interactions between the form, content and contexts of the text and those engaging with it. In the case of a playtext, the latter will include not only the readers or audience, but also the creative team and the actors. As will also become clear from this Element's sections, I am more interested in identifying theatrical processes in playtexts. Their meaning will continue to be open to debate.

A Troubled Term

Theatricality has been approached from a number of perspectives, and I will provide a brief survey here and in the following section, both to distinguish the different approaches from each other and to reflect on their utility as analytical tools. A frequent problem with the term is that its meaning is somehow assumed to be a given and so some scholars fail to provide a definition in the first place.[3] In addition, scholarly disagreement has meant that no single definition has ever been agreed upon, as Thomas Postlewait and Tracy C. David indicate: 'Such a definition [. . .] would offer some much-needed clarity to a very confused situation, but the domain of theatricality cannot be located within any single definition, period, or practice.'[4]

Discourse on theatricality starts with Plato and his attacks on theatre[5] and continues off and on thereafter.[6] However, academic engagements with 'theatricality' start to emerge with the establishment of the study of theatre around the turn of the twentieth century. They were pioneered by Nikolai Evreinov, who published a series of works between 1912 and 1924 that were collected in English as *The Theatre in Life* in 1927. I will return to his ideas in the final section of the Introduction.

Around the middle of the twentieth century, it is sociologists rather than theatre scholars who began to probe theatre as a metaphor for the ways that people interact in society, suggesting that they exhibited aspects of theatricality. The best known was Erving Goffman, who wrote *The Presentation of Self in Everyday Life* (1959). Here, he uses theatrical metaphors such as 'stage', 'character', and 'audience' to describe social interactions, but, by the end of

---

[3] Remarkably, for example, Martin Puchner offers no definition of the term in a section called 'The Invention of Theatricality', the introduction to his book *Stage Fright: Modernism, Anti-Theatricality & Drama* (Baltimore: Johns Hopkins University Press, 2002), pp. 1–28.

[4] Thomas Postlewait and Tracy C. Davis, 'Theatricality: An Introduction', in Davis and Postlewait (eds.), *Theatricality* (Cambridge: Cambridge University Press, 2003), pp. 1–39 (3).

[5] For an excellent discussion and interpretation of Plato's argument, see Samuel Weber, *Theatricality as Medium* (New York: Fordham University Press, 2004), pp. 3–10.

[6] See Jonas Barish, *The Antitheatrical Prejudice* (Berkeley: University of California Press, 1981) for the classic account of the many and various criticisms of 'the theatrical' on stage and beyond.

the study, notes that 'it should be admitted that this attempt to press a mere analogy so far was in part a rhetoric and a manoeuvre'.[7] In short, Goffman exposes the limitations of his own approach: a metaphor will always break down because it is not an analytical, but an associative category. All the world is clearly not a stage in any literal sense.

Theatricality was confronted head-on in Elizabeth Burns' book of the same name. Here, she introduces some key ideas that will feature in subsequent discussions:

> the understanding of theatricality depends on the perception of the two-way process whereby drama in performance is both formed by and helps to re-form and so conserve or change the values and norms of the society which supports it.[8]

Her approach hinges on the act of performance, but the performance itself has to be a special kind of performance so that theatrical elements can be perceived as such; it must be, in some way, ostentatious. She goes on to offer a non-essentialist understanding of theatricality: 'Behaviour is not [...] theatrical because it is of a certain kind but because the observer recognises certain patterns and sequences which are analogous to those with which he [*sic*] is familiar in the theatre'.[9] That is, as the theatre changes, so do the categories of theatricality in any given culture. This position is historically relative and depends on both the specific contexts in which theatricality is identified and the means through which it is exposed.

While Burns seeks to connect theatre and society in what she calls 'the two-way process', theatre scholars have been more focused on what makes theatre theatrical. Critical theorist Roland Barthes offered a simple formula: 'it is theater-minus-text [...]; it is that ecumenical perception of sensuous artifice'.[10] Two of the most influential international theatre researchers, Patrice Pavis and Hans-Thies Lehmann, agreed with Barthes that theatricality was, as Willmar Sauter puts it, 'mainly the business of directors. Within this definition, theatricality is more or less equivalent to what other scholars call *mise-en-scène*'.[11] Erika Fischer-Lichte elaborates on the four categories

---

[7] Irving Goffman, *The Presentation of Self in Everyday Life* (London: Penguin, 1969), pp. 9 and 246, respectively.

[8] Elizabeth Burns, *Theatricality. A Study of Convention in the Theatre and in Social Life* (New York: Harper & Row, 1972), pp. 3–4.

[9] Ibid., p. 12.

[10] Roland Barthes, 'Baudelaire's Theater', in Barthes, *Critical Essays*, tr. by Richard Howard (Evanston: Northwestern University Press, 1972), pp. 25–31 (26). Here and elsewhere, I have retained US English spellings.

[11] Willmar Sauter, *The Theatrical Event. Dynamics of Performance and Perception* (Iowa City: University of Iowa Press, 2000), p. 51.

required for theatricality to be invoked,[12] here neatly summarized by Andreas Kotte: 'The effect of the situation (performance) that develops from interacting bodies (corporality) is also recognized (perception), due to being structured in a particular way (production).'[13] Janelle Reinelt provides further commentary: 'reception is central [to Fischer-Lichte], since she believes that spectators must perceive that the process of using signs as signs prevails over their customary semiotic function in order for the process to be theatrical'.[14] Again, Burns' emphasis on a clear perception of performance finds itself embedded in these ideas.

Fischer-Lichte's attempts to define theatricality also hinge on the ways that the theatre uses signs: 'theatricality may be defined as a particular mode of using signs or as a particular kind of semiotic process in which particular signs (human beings and objects of their environment) are employed as signs of signs'.[15] That is, any given society produces particular signs and distinguishes itself from others in doing so. Theatre then reproduces these signs on stage. However, as Postlewait and Davis note, an attempt to systematize theatricality with reference to signs and their usage failed because the semioticians assumed 'that the dramatic and performance texts, with their thousands and thousands of signs, could be described as if there were one ideal spectator who would (or should) see and read all the signs (in accordance with the semiotician's model)'.[16] As such, this scientistic approach revealed itself to be something of a dead-end.

To conclude, briefly: scholars' engagement with the category of theatricality is broad and varied, to say the least. Some have tried to keep it locked in theatres, others to assay metaphorical connections to our everyday lives. At the heart of the matter is a problem of definition, and I will offer my own in the final section of the Introduction.

However, before moving on and because I am concerned with what playtexts might tell us about theatricality, a consideration of metatheatre may help us understand the connection between the two. Lionel Abel coined the term in 1963, primarily for plays, and Martin Puchner points out, 'Abel observes that

---

[12] Erika Fischer-Lichte, 'Verwandlung als ästhetische Kategorie. Zur Entwicklung einer neuen Ästhetik des Performativen', in Fischer-Lichte, Friedemann Kreuder and Isabel Pflug (eds.), *Theater seit den 60er Jahren. Grenzgänge der Neo-Avantgarde* (Tübingen: A Franke, 1998), pp. 21–91 (88).

[13] Andreas Kotte, *Studying Theatre. Phenomena, Structures and Functions* (Vienna: Lit Verlag, 2010), pp. 231–2.

[14] Janelle Reinelt, 'The Politics of Discourse: Performativity Meets Theatricality', *SubStance*, 31: 2&3 (2002), pp. 201–15 (208).

[15] Erika Fischer-Lichte, 'Theatricality: A Key Concept in Theatre and Cultural Studies', *Theatre Research International*, 20: 2 (1995), pp. 85–9 (88).

[16] Postlewait and Davis, 'Theatricality: An Introduction', p. 25.

the term *metatheatre* is a subset of what should be called theatricality'.[17] Richard Hornby offers a clear definition: 'metadrama can be defined as drama about drama; it occurs whenever the subject of a play turns out to be, in some sense, drama itself'.[18] The implications of this position have been much debated.

Abel roots his understanding of metaplays in self-consciousness:

> all of them are theatre pieces about life seen as already theatricalized. By this I mean that the persons appearing on the stage [. . .] knew they were dramatic before the playwright took note of them. What dramatized them originally? Myth, legend, past literature, they themselves.[19]

Abel proceeds from an interesting position: that life has already been pervaded by the theatrical, although he locates its source in literature and self-awareness. He adds that 'in the metaplay there will always be a fantastic element', suggesting that theatricality can only manifest itself in the playtext through features not found in our everyday experiences.[20] I will dispute this idea in the Conclusion.

Hornby takes a more pragmatic approach and lists certain features of a metadrama: the play within the play; the ceremony within the play; role-playing within the role; literary and real-life references; and self-reference.[21] These all point to the play's own constructedness and dispel any sense that the play is in some way an unproblematic representation of an external reality. They also draw our attention to how plays might work in that, for example, in a play within a play, 'the relationship of the inner play to the outer play prefigures the relationship between the outer play and the reality within which it occurs: life', as Robert J. Nelson explains.[22]

Mark Ringer suggests three functions of self-consciousness in the metatheatrical playtext:

> it served to express the depth of the play world; it defined the relationship of that world with the reality represented by the audience; and, finally this self-referential art allowed members of the audience to recognize the elements of illusion present in their daily lives.[23]

---

[17] Martin Puchner, 'Introduction', in Lionel Abel, *Tragedy and Metatheatre. Essays on Dramatic Form*, introduced by Martin Puchner (NY: Holmes and Meyer, 2003), pp. 1–24 (11).

[18] Richard Hornby, *Drama, Metadrama, and Perception* (London: Associated Universities Presses, 1986), p. 31.

[19] Lionel Abel, *Tragedy and Metatheatre. Essays on Dramatic Form*, introduced by Martin Puchner (NY: Holmes and Meyer, 2003), p. 134.

[20] Ibid., p. 153.   [21] Ibid., p. 32.

[22] Robert J. Nelson, *Play within a Play. The Dramatist's Conception of His Art: Shakespeare to Anouilh* (New Haven: Yale University Press, 1958), p. 10.

[23] Mark Ringer, *Electra and the Empty Urn. Metatheater and Role Playing in Sophocles* (Chapel Hill: University of North Carolina Press, 1998), p. 12.

A dialogue between stage and auditorium is clear, especially in the final observation. Here, self-consciousness allows spectators to connect theatrical processes with those experienced outside the theatre. Postlewait and Davis add an extra feature, in that the

> metatheatrical condition also served as a counter-challenge to theatre's detractors who condemned the stage for its dissembling inauthenticity, for if it acknowledged its own terms of engagement, denying an expectation of belief, it cut detractors off at the knees.[24]

This openness, showing the workings, as it were, of the theatrical process, is understood as a key moment in a defence against antitheatricality, but also, when coupled with Ringer's final point, gestures towards why I am studying theatricality rather than metatheatre in this Element: theatricality extends beyond the theatre and asks some difficult questions about the nature of our social existence.

A Troubling Term

It may be difficult to find a single term associated with the theatre that does not appear in common English. People are accused of putting on an act; an event may be stage-managed; accidents are called tragedies; the curtain falls on a notable life. As Jonas Barish notes: 'with infrequent exceptions [as are my last two examples], terms borrowed from the theater [...] tend to be hostile or belittling'.[25] Our language pays testament to the difficulties of differentiating real life from theatre, and how real life seeks to distance itself from the pretence associated with theatre by disparaging the persistence of the theatre's presence beyond the stage. I suggest that the bridge between the theatre and life is represented by this Element's focus, theatricality.

The question of where theatricality starts and stops is a crucial one. For sociologists interested in the theatrical features of everyday life, metaphors allowed them to explore theatricality's reach without wholeheartedly committing to a too literal implementation of their ideas. Richard Schechner states that while Goffman provided the foundation for the edifice that became Performance Studies, he 'did not propose that "all the world's a stage", a notion which implies a kind of falseness or put on'.[26] The limits of the

---

[24] Postlewait and Davis, 'Theatricality: An Introduction', p. 15.

[25] Barish, *The Antitheatrical Prejudice*, p. 1.

[26] Richard Schechner, *Performance Theory*, revised and expanded edition (London: Routledge, 2003), p. x.

metaphor help Schechner recover a sense of dignity and sincerity in everyday life.

The philosopher Bruce Wilshire also felt threatened by the prospect that the quotidian world was little more than an extended theatre. He is prepared to concede that, in public, the self plays roles and is subject to processes encountered in the theatre. His boundary, however, is what he calls 'offstage', more private moments with, say, loved ones or family, out of the gaze of others. He sets out the terms of the challenge of a pervasive theatricality, in that he seeks to test

> if an independent account of the conditions of identity of self offstage tends to confirm the convictions we hold in the theatre. If these conditions of identity turn out to be *theatre-like* then theatre as metaphor will have an excellent chance to grasp them. Of course, if theatrical metaphor in all its versions and ramifications turns out to be essential, then a strictly independent account of the conditions of identity of self will be impossible.[27]

The possibility that one is always performing undermines Wilshire's individualist position: 'The engrossing pursuit of authenticity lies in advancing and perfecting our individual reality.'[28] The reference to authenticity seeks to differentiate, like Schechner, between theatrical pretence and lived realness. I will revisit the problematic category of authenticity as a political issue in the Conclusion.

Fischer-Lichte is also keen to delimit theatricality by placing it solely within the confines of the theatre. Reinelt, who quotes an unpublished work by the scholar, states:

> Recognizing that theatricality applies to theater and to processes in culture and in everyday life, [Fischer-Lichte] wants to keep from blurring them together: 'For, if everything is "theatre", the concept becomes so wide that it loses any distinctive or cognitive capacity.'[29]

Here, the restriction comes from an anxiety concerning the utility of a term that can entirely permeate both the stage and the society that surrounds it; that it loses all meaning if it is to be found everywhere. I will return to this conundrum, later in this Element.

Another theatre scholar who has made a continued contribution to the study of theatricality is Josette Féral. She develops some interesting ideas that inevitably extend the applicability of theatricality beyond the stage. She begins by asking a fundamental question, a 'which comes first?': does theatricality

---

[27] Bruce Wilshire, *Role Playing and Identity: The Limits of Theatre as Metaphor* (Bloomington: Indiana University Press, 1982), pp. 138–9.
[28] Ibid., pp. 221–2.   [29] Reinelt, 'The Politics of Discourse', p. 207.

pervade the world or does it emerge from the theatre?[30] She then notes that
a spectator can contemplate a stage set, empty of actors, and realize that it is
different from reality, deriving the conclusion that 'space is the vehicle of
theatricality'.[31]

William Eggington elucidates this claim in his study of the conditions under
which theatricality escaped the trappings of the stage. The argument opens with
his approval of the Spanish cultural historian Emilio Orozco Díaz, who
'describes Baroque space as involving a dynamic of profundity and the ten-
dency of the spectacle to penetrate into the space reserved for the audience – he
sees it, in other words, as the increased fluidity between spaces, the overflow of
theatrical into real space'.[32] So, at this moment of theatre history, the stage is in
such an intense dialogue with the auditorium that it is difficult to differentiate
between the two. He continues:

> The constitution of a frame separating realities that are nevertheless suscep-
> tible to interpenetration and mise en abîme, *precisely because the spaces that
> comprise them are mimetically related*, is an essential characteristic of
> theatricality.[33]

As such, attempts to separate the stage from the auditorium and spaces beyond it
are doomed to fail, and one has to accept that the representations one sees on
stage may overlap with one's encounters elsewhere.

With this fluid sense of space in mind, Féral then observes that a person
outside the theatre may observe theatrical qualities in someone who is not
consciously exhibiting them,[34] perhaps in a certain way of speaking
a sentence or making a gesture. She draws the conclusion:

> theatricality appears to be more than a property; in fact, we might call it
> a process that recognizes subjects in process; it is a process of looking at or
> being looked at. It is an act initiated in one of two possible spaces: either that
> of the actor or that of the spectator.[35]

As it happens, Féral's conclusion agrees with Nikolai Evreinov, the theorist
writing in the early twentieth century:

> The art of the theatre is pre-aesthetic, and not aesthetic, for the simple reason
> that *transformation*, which is after all the essence of all theatrical art, is more

[30] See Josette Féral, 'Theatricality: The Specificity of Theatrical Language', *SubStance*, 31: 2&3
(2002), pp. 94–108 (95).
[31] Ibid., p. 96.
[32] William Eggington, *How the World Became a Stage: Presence, Theatricality and the Question of
Modernity* (Albany, NY: State University of New York Press, 2003), pp. 78–9.
[33] Ibid., p. 79.   [34] Féral, 'Theatricality', p. 97.   [35] Ibid., p. 98.

primitive and more easily attainable than *formation*, which is the essence of aesthetic arts.[36]

Féral argues her position more cogently, but both commentators appreciate that theatricality was not the creation of the theatre, but its prerequisite. This is radical and justifies the anxieties considered earlier: theatricality precedes theatre and is thus primarily a social category, and we will have to deal with that in some way.

A New Approach

In his own survey of theatricality, Sauter categorizes scholars' ideas under four headings. He calls them '*metaphoric*', '*descriptive*', '*binary*' and '*epochal*'.[37] I have already discussed the first one, and indeed the second, which he ascribes to Barthes, Pavis and Lehmann. The third is the attempt made to differentiate between the theatrical and the non-theatrical, as expressed by Wilshire, and the fourth seeks to define theatricality in relative terms, according to the particular place and time of the study, as Burns advocated and Eggington identified as starting in the Baroque period. I would like to add a fifth category, one that I hope will address some of the shortcomings I have already identified and offer a straightforward method to readers seeking to explore manifestations of theatricality in the playtext.

My new category is 'materialist'. Rather than attempting to define the qualities of theatricality, I prefer to return to Evreinov's day when the Russian linguist Roman Jakobson wanted to identify *literaturnost,* the 'literariness' of literary text. As Barrett Watten comments: 'Jakobson's scientistic definition of literaturnost positioned literature as an object of knowledge in a way that would lead to the institution of norms'.[38] While it might sound a little old-fashioned, I am seeking to identify the 'theatreness' of the theatre. This I trace back not to qualities, but to four material *processes* that constitute the performance of a playtext:

- Actors play roles
- Actors speak the words of others
- Actors are given instructions by others
- Actors perform to live audiences

---

[36] Evreinov, quoted in Kotte, *Studying Theatre*, p. 229.
[37] Sauter, *The Theatrical Event*, pp. 51–2.
[38] Barrett Watten, 'The Bride of the Assembly Line. Radical Poetics in Construction', in Maria Damon and Ira Livingston (eds.), *Poetry and Cultural Studies. A Reader* (Chicago: University of Illinois Press, 2009, pp. 163–76 (165).

While the processes are plain, evident and perhaps even banal for anyone who has engaged in making theatre, their implications beyond the stage, following Evreinov and Féral, are far-reaching and profound. That is, in part, because much is done to repress a recognition of their presence in everyday life. As Burns states, for example, 'Few people like to believe that they are acting all the time. This seems to be perceived as a charge of insincerity and even a denial of identity.'[39] I will address the repercussions of this point in the next section. Here, however, I will merely note that each process has significant implications for the ways that we lead our lives, given that theatricality precedes the theatre and that its processes originate in society, not on the stage.

Positing these four processes as existing not only in theatrical production but in the production of everyday relationships and behaviours suggests that they are trans-historical and essential, two terms that any scholar is wary of using because of the universality they imply. Indeed, they also lead one to the conclusion that theatricality is everywhere, a position that Fischer-Lichte seeks to avoid: 'For, if everything is "theatre", the concept becomes so wide that it loses any distinctive or cognitive capacity.'[40] The question thus arises as to what one is to do if the concept *is* so broad and all-encompassing.

We are no longer in a position simply to point to a phenomenon and glibly announce that 'it's theatre' as if that had some meaning in itself. Instead, theatricality, as expressed in the four processes, takes a great many forms, and it is the job of the analyst to detect the processes, identify their particular configurations and interactions with each other, and draw conclusions for both the playtext and its wider meanings for society from the specificity of the representations. And this, broadly speaking, is the method I offer the reader in the rest of this Element.

Before moving on to the structure of the sections, I want to note the care taken in phrasing the four processes. That is, actors do not necessarily play characters, a term that is too laden with specific cultural associations, but roles, a term I will define in the next section. And if people play roles in everyday life, as I will argue, then the term 'actor' applies to each individual in society. In the second process, actors do not deliver the content of scripts because that term is more difficult to apply outside the theatre and is associated with the metaphors applied to theatricality.[41] Instead, I choose the formulation that actors speak

---

[39] Burns, *Theatricality*, p. 20.

[40] Fischer-Lichte, quoted in Reinelt, 'The Politics of Discourse', p. 207. Postlewait and Davis agree, claiming that theatricality 'is a sign empty of meaning; it is the meaning of all signs', in 'Theatricality: An Introduction', p. 1.

[41] See, for example, Burns, *Theatricality*, p. 4, who notes the limits of the metaphor as there is no literal script that people speak in everyday life.

the words of others. In keeping with my materialist approach, I am keen to avoid metaphor and prefer to consider real processes. The third process avoids the term 'director' because this figure is a relatively recent addition to the creative staff.[42] It nonetheless acknowledges that actors have been given instructions throughout the history of the theatre. Ancient Greek choruses did not simply get up and perform, and Elizabethan actors did not take to the stage without rehearsal. Actors have always been told, directly or indirectly, how to go about the business of acting. And I take the fourth process to be straightforward, although it should be noted that it differentiates theatre from other more contemporary forms of recorded performance in which actors are no longer present when the work is shown.

The four processes also allow analysts of playtexts to approach any of the metatheatrical features, identified by Hornby, in a more granular manner. That is, when considering the play within a play, for example, one can investigate how actors play roles, how they speak the words of others, the instructions they may receive, and how they perform before a live onstage audience. Each instance of this device will differ, however markedly or subtly, between different playtexts, and so by examining its component processes, the reader can apprehend how they work together to establish their potential effects and meanings. In addition, paying attention to metatheatrical devices as itemized by Hornby can help us understand how the theatrical processes might work in any given playtext.

Each section will deal with each process in turn and will engage with two playtexts as examples of contrasting ways of treating each process. Of course, focussing on a single process in each playtext should not suggest that other processes are neither present nor visible, and some of the examples will reference other processes in their arguments. It is also worth differentiating between overt and covert theatrical processes. The sections will mostly focus on overt instances. Yet, as noted, theatrical processes in everyday life often present themselves as covert. And while this distinction serves broadly as a rule of thumb, there are certainly exceptions to this rule and I will point them out as they arise.

There is also, of course, a very large choice of candidate playtexts available to illustrate a particular process, and my choices represent only two exemplars of each. In Section 1, I examine *Heart's Desire* by Caryl Churchill and *Fires in the Mirror* by Anna Deavere Smith because they treat the notion of role-play quite

---

[42] Peter M. Boenisch dates the first recorded German-speaking director back to 1771, a revision of around 100 years from its usual starting point with the Duke of Saxe-Meiningen in the 1870s, in *Directing Scenes and Senses. The Thinking of 'Regie'* (Manchester: Manchester University Press, 2015), pp. 16–9.

differently and do not foreground characters consciously playing roles in their dramaturgy. Section 2 contrasts a play that systematically charts the process of language acquisition, *Kaspar* by Peter Handke, with Churchill's *Blue Kettle*, where the two words of the play's title unexpectedly invade apparently conventional dialogue. Section 3 takes *Catastrophe* by Samuel Beckett as an example of what happens when an actor deliberately defies a director. It then considers *The Decision* by Bertolt Brecht as a play set outside a theatre where a central figure is unable to carry out instructions despite wanting to. Section 4 investigates *Eumenides* by Aeschylus as a classic example of explicitly inviting an audience's judgement. Jackie Sibblies Drury's *Fairview*, on the other hand, turns the tables on the audience, making it the subject of the play in its final pages, having increasingly unsettled it over time. I discuss my choice of Ibsen's *Ghosts* in the Conclusion itself. Each analysis proceeds from detecting the presence of at least one theatrical process in the playtext, but crucially seeks to understand their broader ramifications in society, providing a link between theatre and the world beyond it.

As is clear, there is a decidedly Western flavour to the playtexts under discussion. This is due to my own knowledge of the cultures and their contexts. A productive test of my claims to universalism would be the applicability of the four processes to playtexts beyond Europe and North America, theatres with which I am mostly unfamiliar.

The Conclusion will then ask whether every playtext is actually theatrical, even if it does not exhibit one or more of the four processes explicitly. By analysing a playtext that satisfies this criterion, I will seek to show what that might reveal, not only about the playtext, but its implications for the world beyond the stage.

By the end of this Element, the reader should be familiar with a method for investigating any playtext for overt evidence or covert traces of theatricality's four processes, to process their possible meanings, and to speculate on how they might speak to our everyday lives. The approach I have taken exploits society's innate theatricality as a prerequisite for the theatre's and treats its presence in playtexts as indicative of wider, concrete social issues. As such, the conclusion draws parallels between the artifice of the theatre and the constructedness of social relations, proposing that the latter may be far more changeable than discourses of permanence and inevitability, promoted by capitalist ideologies, might suggest.

Unlike Ludwig Wittgenstein, who believed that he had solved philosophy's problems with his *Tractatus Logico-Philosophicus* in 1918, I do not see this contribution as definitively ending the debates about theatricality. However, it was written in the hope of inviting further engagement with a topic whose importance cannot be understated.

1 Actors Play Roles

Role Call

As noted in the Introduction, a desire to demarcate real life from theatre arises from an anxiety that real life shares the processes that turn a playtext into a production. Theatricality, as I have defined it, however, proposes that the same processes that constitute theatre also constitute real life, and the central process is that actors play roles.

First, it is worth discussing what a role might actually be. Robert J. Landy offers this helpful definition: 'Role is a basic unit of personality containing specific qualities that provide uniqueness and coherence to that unit.'[43] The play of uniqueness and coherence fits well into the social roles we play and roles actors play on stage: the coherence references the broad nature of a role, say, that of a teacher, while the uniqueness represents the ways that we receive and respond to that role – every teacher is different in their own way. Where roles come from is another matter: the role of a teacher will be different in different times and places, and so the answer is going to be found in the social circumstances of any given situation.

The fact that actors play roles is hardly controversial, but what about the more covert role-play suggested by theatricality's presence in everyday life? If I were to ask a parent, a friend, an employer and my partner to describe me in three adjectives, it is unlikely that they would offer the same three words. The reason for this is quite simple: different social situations permit, tolerate and forbid certain behaviours, actions and speech, and we usually pick up on these and act accordingly. Such an example counters Wilshire's belief that we perform when we are 'onstage', but that we do not when we are 'offstage',[44] because there *is* no offstage – the private sphere is still governed by social rules. Each society has an idea of what makes a good parent, for example.

Even the realm of our own heads, which would appear as private as one could get, is not left untouched by the process of role-play. Declan Donnellan's acting pedagogy offers a useful perspective here. He dismisses the term 'character' for fear that it evokes something singular and replaces it with 'identity', which he defines as 'how we see ourselves'. He thus already puts a distance between the observer and oneself, even though they are one and the same person. He goes on

---

[43] Robert J. Landy, *Persona and Performance. The Meaning of Role in Drama, Therapy, and Everyday Life* (London: Jessica Kingsley, 1993), p. 7.
[44] Wilshire, *Role Playing and Identity*, p. 280.

to state that 'the identity is a construction that helps me define who the "I" is when I talk'.[45] He concludes his idea by suggesting that however we might describe ourselves, there is an inverted version of that quality inside ourselves, too. So, in his example of Othello, this figure may see himself as noble and loyal, yet these two qualities are undone at the end of the play. We play roles in our own heads, so that even 'offstage' is an 'onstage', too.

Clearly, the idea that we *only* play roles has implications for who we are, and there are, broadly speaking, two basic ways of approaching this contention. Goffman presents one: that there is a sovereign self controlling the performance of the roles we play: 'I assume that when an individual appears before others he [sic] will have many motives for trying to control the impression they receive of the situation.'[46] Here, he believes that role-playing is always conscious, and that a self is continually making choices. Yet Goffman's retention of a controlling self is not enough for Wilshire: '"role theory" [à la Goffman] leaves us finally without guidance concerning what we are to make of ourselves and how we are to move within a world which we must make our own in one way or another'.[47] Here, Wilshire is displaying his existentialist belief in an altogether more sovereign self, capable of autonomous self-determination. Barish explains: 'We may fulfill ourselves either authentically or inauthentically; we may opt (in the sociologist's jargon) for "role-making" or "role-taking".'[48] Here, 'role-making' is an act of will, driven by the self.

Landy, on the other hand, states that:

> Role is an essential concept that provides coherence to the personality and in many ways supersedes the primacy of the concept of self. A full understanding of role implies an understanding of the essentially dramatic aspects of everyday existence.[49]

He suggests that all we have is role-play, and later that personalities are people's 'role systems'.[50] The sheer number of roles we play implies that we do not play roles consciously all the time. Roles are often absorbed and developed unconsciously; diners are not explicitly told how to behave in a restaurant, pedestrians not how to walk on a pavement, students not how to behave in a lecture. Individuals observe different social situations and act accordingly, or not. Modification and transgression of the rules will be discussed in Sections 3 and 4. The unconscious adoption of roles makes them less identifiable and more covert.

---

[45] Declan Donnellan, *The Actor and the Target* (London: Nick Hern, 2002), all quotations p. 100.
[46] Goffman, *The Presentation of Self*, p. 26.   [47] Wilshire, p. 283.
[48] Barish, *The Antitheatrical Prejudice*, p. 476.   [49] Landy, *Persona and Performance*, p. 7.
[50] Ibid., pp. 36–7.

The proposition that we always only play roles is both convincing and unsettling. It convinces for two main reasons. First, that we are never beyond the gaze of the other and are consequently always performing to someone, even if that someone is oneself. Second, that we can perform unconsciously, slipping between roles that we may not have chosen to play. The proposition is unsettling because the self has been replaced by what Landy has called 'role systems', an interactive aggregation of roles that give an identity its coherence. These roles are not essential to the person; circumstances can change and a role one may have played for years may no longer be tenable or desirable.

The proposition that we only ever play roles is a distinctly double-edged sword. Having no core may well lead a person to ask who they are, what they have to hold on to at points of crisis. On the other hand, this prospect can fill a person with hope: what if one is not the failure that poor exam results suggested, or not the vile racist who was sent to prison for hate crimes? When one reaches a certain age, one can look back at all the constructions of self that one has made and see how they have transformed as times have changed.

A further ramification of being self less, one that derives its menace from the theatre, is that actors are not their roles; they pretend. If we always only play roles, are we never able to behave with integrity or with sincerity? Are those qualities only pretence? Postlewait and Davis offer some comfort:

> Mimesis may not mislead, because when caught up by it, the actors and spectators agree to forgo truth. This 'mimetic conundrum' implies that performers and spectators are still true to themselves, though paradoxically the representation may lack truth.[51]

The idea of being 'caught up' by a role, of playing it less consciously, or of being aware of it and choosing to play it with integrity or sincerity is underwritten by a knowledge of the ontological situation, that all we have is role-play. We still have the concept of honesty, which presumes that such a virtue can still be accessed while playing a role, bearing out Postlewait and Davis's proposition. Of course, insincerity and deceit are also parts of the roles we play. More often than not, we are aware when we are lying or being devious. These, too, are potential options for the role player, but they are also inflected with a negative value in most social situations (although, e.g., undercover agents who infiltrate criminal activity could still be considered to be acting with integrity when upholding the democratic rule of law). Role-play does not, then, imply that everything is pretence and has no meaning. Rather, actions have consequences and interact with moral codes, which nonetheless change over time.

---

[51] Postlewait and Davis, 'Theatricality: An Introduction', p. 6.

The subsequent examination of two very different playtexts will proceed from the position that we always only play roles and consider its implications in the theatre before considering what that might mean outside of it.

Caryl Churchill, *Heart's Desire*

Heart's Desire (premiere 1997) is a decidedly odd play. It seeks to tell an apparently humdrum story of a mother, Alice, and a father, Brian, awaiting the return of their daughter, Susy. Brian's sister, Maisie, is also in attendance, and the couple's son, Lewis, enters drunk on a couple of occasions, too. The oddness comes from a series of 'resets', that is, an action takes place and at a particular moment, the action stops and restarts at an earlier point in the plot. The very opening introduces this idea: Brian enters, putting on a red sweater, says 'She's taking her time', to which Alice replies 'Not really',[52] before the action resets to exactly the same scene, yet Brian is putting on a tweed jacket. The same thing happens again, but this time, Brian puts on an old cardigan and the action continues until the next reset.

From the very start, we see the same figures performing the same tasks, but with a slight variation. R. Darren Gobert suggests that the choice of the old cardigan as the one that allows the plot to continue marks Brian as an elderly father better than the other costume choices.[53] He thus points to the play's metatheatricality, that the performance will only proceed when it conforms to a theatrically appropriate solution. The next reset may support this interpretation: Maisie engages in a lengthy speech about how she envies Susy for living in Australia because its fauna have taken a completely different evolutionary path. On the one hand, the speech is unprovoked and it is long, two qualities that may prevent it from satisfying the criterion of appropriateness. On the other, a woman is talking positively about alterity: there is a political dimension to the speech that has been cut off before it could conclude. Daniel Jernigan provides an apposite reason for the resets: 'a closer reading of *Heart's Desire* reveals that many of the narrative disruptions directly comment on power relations between men and women'.[54] He does, however, qualify the mechanism with the word 'many'. I will return to the cause of the resets later in this section.

---

[52] Caryl Churchill, *Heart's Desire*, in Churchill, *Plays*, volume 4 (London: Nick Hern, 2008), pp. 63–95 (65). Subsequent references to the playtext will appear as bracketed page numbers in the main text.

[53] See R. Darren Gobert, 'On Performance and Selfhood in Caryl Churchill', in Elaine Aston and Elin Diamond, *The Cambridge Companion to Caryl Churchill* (Cambridge: Cambridge University Press, 2009), pp. 105–24 (116).

[54] Daniel Jernigan, '*Traps, Softcops, Blue Heart* and *This Is a Chair*: Tracking Epistemological Upheaval in Caryl Churchill's Shorter Plays', *Modern Drama*, 47: 1 (2004), pp. 21–43 (26).

The playtext's time-traveling dramaturgy draws attention to the figures' role play. For example, the next reset is precipitated by the following exchange:

BRIAN: It's so delightful for you always being so right.
ALICE: That's it. I'm leaving. (66)

In the subsequent iteration, we find:

BRIAN: It's so delightful for you always being so right.
ALICE: She didn't want to be met. (68)

Alice is playing her role as a wife differently. In the first example, Brian's sarcasm leads Alice to abandon the family home. In the second, Alice has modified her behaviour and grown a thicker skin, allowing the plot to continue. This would appear to accord with Jernigan's contention: 'In each case, the scene is reset to earlier, more acceptable, moments, in which the patriarchy is firmly in control.'[55] Subsequent resets, however, call this reason for the modification of role into question.

On three occasions, Brian and Alice's drunken son Lewis enters. Twice, Brian contributes to his removal. First, he curses Lewis's very existence, wishing that he had died at birth. Second, Brian simply, but insistently orders him 'Out' (84). If the patriarchy were 'firmly in control', the playtext would have permitted Brian both to continue his hate-filled speech and endorse Lewis's expulsion. But just like Alice, he, too, is required to play his role as father differently when the scene is reset. And there are further resets that also call Jernigan's explanation into question.

The sequence of events seems to have reached its conclusion when Susy finally appears and says, 'Mummy. Daddy. How wonderful to be home' (86). This is a curious point at which to reset as it would seem that the plot has resolved itself and the wait is over. Gobert considers 'her frankly undramatic opening line [as] lacking in agonistic grist'.[56] Enric Monforte Rabascall makes a similar point: 'This is a totally idealised version of a coming home'.[57] Both note a metadramatic regulation in play here – the line disappoints the sense of a drama. Later, Susy appears again, as if for the first time, and Brian declares, 'You are my heart's desire' (92), which leads to another reset. Critics have noted an incest theme here,[58] and this accounts for the final, approved version of the action. That is, by the end of the playtext, the figures appear to be playing the

---

[55] Ibid.

[56] R. Darren Gobert, *The Theatre of Caryl Churchill* (London: Bloomsbury, 2014), p. 182.

[57] Enric Monforte Rabascall, *Gender, Politics, Subjectivity: Reading Caryl Churchill* (unpublished doctoral thesis: University of Barcelona, 2000), p. 270.

[58] See, for example, ibid., p. 271 and Gobert, *The Theatre of Caryl Churchill*, p. 186.

roles ascribed to them and the speeches that we have read so many times reach their conclusion. Except that as Brian says, 'You are my heart's –,' he is interrupted and the performance resets one final time.

In her introduction to the play, Churchill notes, '*Heart's Desire* is a play that can't happen, obsessively resetting itself back to the beginning every time it veers off course.'[59] The question arises as to whose course she is talking about. I have already considered Jernigan's point that patriarchal values are the determining factor and Gobert's that the actions adhere to certain dramatic norms that cannot be derailed. I prefer to combine both proposals and suggest that British middle-class values are moderating the action, in both the relations between the sexes and the propriety of the theatre. I offer a couple more examples of some of the more unexpected moments as evidence.

Following Gobert, I agree that the transgression of genre leads to numerous resets, such as when gunmen kill all on stage, and when this domestic drama unexpectedly becomes a whodunnit. Gobert also detects an 'irruption of the real',[60] as Hans-Thies Lehmann puts it in his foundational study of postdramatic theatre, when a '*horde of small children rush in, round the room and out again*' (74). Here, Gobert notes how an internal memo within the Royal Court Theatre ordered an offstage 'corralling of the children', due to their exuberance onstage.[61] That is, the children, who were only playing their own boisterous selves, broke the rules of dramatic theatre and thus had to be banished.

And as I have noted, the values of the actions performed on stage are those of the polite middle class, at home in a domestic setting. The patriarch is not allowed to rail against his son, and he certainly cannot express his incestuous heart's desire. Likewise, after one of the resets, an official knocks on the door and demands to see the family's papers, leading Maisie to fear that she will be removed from the house. The scene resets, and the official is never seen again because his role represents an extreme society, and middle-class families cannot have their homes invaded by threatening bureaucrats.

Gobert notes that *Heart's Desire* 'likens its own setting to a stage or rehearsal room populated by absurd repetitions'.[62] That is, Churchill exploits metatheatricality to undermine the individual figures' sovereignty. They find themselves at the mercy of situations that the bourgeois stage and its representations find unacceptable and continually have to adapt for the play to reach a conclusion.

---

[59] Caryl Churchill, 'Introduction', in Churchill, *Plays*, volume 4 (London: Nick Hern, 2008), pp. vii–x (vii).

[60] See Hans-Thies Lehmann, *Postdramatic Theatre*, tr. by Karen Jürs-Munby (Abingdon: Routledge, 2006), pp. 99–104.

[61] See Gobert, *The Theatre of Caryl Churchill*, p. 185.

[62] Gobert, 'On Performance and Selfhood', pp. 105–24 (115).

Brian, however, presents a point of resistance: he cannot contain his heart's desire, will not play a more measured role, and thus crashes the plot. Churchill's play is a study of how domestic roles change according to a value system that tyrannically demands moderation in all things.

Anna Deavere Smith, *Fires in the Mirror: Crown Heights, Brooklyn and Other Identities.*

The inspiration, or perhaps provocation for Anna Deavere Smith's *Fires in the Mirror* (premiere 1992), was an incident in the Crown Heights district of Brooklyn, New York City, on 19 August 1991. A car in a motorcade escorting the spiritual leader of the Lubavitch Jewish community drove through a red traffic light, collided with another car, mounted the pavement, killed a seven-year-old Black boy, Gavin Cato, and injured his cousin, Angela, who was teaching him how to ride his bicycle. While this was clearly an accident – the driver did not intend to harm anyone – it was the circumstances under which the accident took place that triggered a response. That is, sections of the Black community saw the Lubavitchers as receiving preferential treatment, denied to them, as the cause of the accident. Violence flared up against the police and Lubavitchers, and later that evening, a young Jewish scholar from Australia, Yankel Rosenbaum, was attacked and killed by a group of young Black men. Full-blown rioting began the next day, the same day that the Lubavitcher driver fled to Israel. The rioting continued for another couple of days.

Smith undertook a series of interviews in the autumn of 1991 with both key, lesser and anonymous figures who witnessed the riots, and with people not directly connected with them. The latter interviews provide contextual perspectives on the riots, mostly in terms of racial politics. The former combine context and eyewitness accounts. The playtext, then, gathers verbatim material, arranging it as a montage of conflicting and contradictory views and opinions. As such, this would appear to differ little from standard practices of verbatim theatre and to have little to do with this section's focus on the theatrical process of actors playing roles and its presence in everyday life.

What differentiates *Fires in the Mirror* from other verbatim plays, however, is the fact that Smith plays all the figures she interviewed on stage.[63] In her introduction to the book edition, she argues for an approach to acting that eschews starting with the actor's self, 'something that led to the diverse characters sounding "the same"',[64] in favour of approaching other people on

---

[63] In the only revival of the play of which I am aware, a single actor, Michael Benjamin Washington, played all the roles in 2019.

[64] Anna Deavere Smith, 'Introduction', in Smith, *Fires in the Mirror: Crown Heights Brooklyn and Other Identities* (New York: Anchor, 1993), pp. xxiii–xli (xxvi).

their own terms: 'I started thinking that if I listened carefully to people's words, and particularly to their rhythms, that I could use language to learn about my own time.'[65] Smith makes an important political point here, opening up a dialectic between individual and society: that the individual is in dialogue with their society and inevitably bears its mark when negotiating it (a point I will explore in greater detail in the next section). She is thus able to undo any semblance of a quality often associated with the performance of documentary material, that we see people 'as they really are'[66] in favour of something quite different. As Debby Thompson notes:

> fundamental to a post-structuralist critique of liberal humanist models of identity is the belief that ideology and ideological state apparati (including the arts) create 'common sense' or 'obviousness' or 'believability'. Ideological state apparati make us experience ideological structures as deeply personal, natural, and instinctive.[67]

That is, Smith performs each authentic voice in such a way that it is denaturalized in order to expose, rather than to repress, the influence of society on the roles that people play. Jill Dolan summarizes Smith's approach to performance thus:

> Smith performs mimicry instead of mimesis [. . .], never pretending to hold a mirror up to life but only to mimic it, pointing to the images she creates of identity as separate from her and from each other, as surrounded by gaps that shouldn't be closed but with which we must always grapple.[68]

The distinction Dolan makes between mimesis and mimicry is significant in that there is a clear distance between performer and performance, a process that opens up a space for dialogue between the two.

Various critics have observed the effects of the acting. Richard Schechner states that 'she does not destroy the others or parody them. Nor does she lose herself',[69] while William H. Sun and Faye C. Fei align her work with Brechtian performance in that she combines representation, distance and critique.[70] The

---

[65] Ibid., p. xxv.

[66] See, for example, Bella Merlin 's Stanislavskian approach to playing real figures in 'Acting Hare. The Permanent Way', in Richard Boon (ed.), *The Cambridge Companion to David Hare* (Cambridge: Cambridge University Press, 2007), pp. 123–37.

[67] Debby Thompson, '"Is race a trope?": Anna Deavere Smith and the Question of Racial Performativity', *African American Review*, 37: 1 (2003), pp. 127–38 (129).

[68] Jill Dolan, '"Finding Our Feet in the Shoes of (One An) Other": Multiple Character Solo Performers and Utopian Performatives', *Modern Drama*, 45: 4 (2002), pp. 495–518 (513).

[69] Richard Schechner, 'Anna Deavere Smith: Acting as Incorporation', *The Drama Review*, 37: 4 (1993), pp. 63–64 (64).

[70] See William H. Sun and Faye C. Fei, 'Masks or Faces Re-Visited: A Study of Four Theatrical Works Concerning Cultural Identity', *The Drama Review*, 38: 4 (1994), pp. 120–32 (130–1).

Brechtian reference point is pertinent because Smith's approach resembles Brecht's 'basic model for an epic theatre', the 'Street Scene' essay. Here, he invites actors not to become their roles, but to show them, to demonstrate the different positions they take up with respect to a common incident, here, uncannily, a car accident. One central criterion applies to each representation: 'the demonstration should have a socially practical significance'.[71] This is not a disagreement about what happened based on individual personalities, but on different subject positions that openly display their 'group memberships',[72] such as gender, class, race, age, ability, religious affiliation and a host of others. Interestingly, Smith was unaware of the essay until a former assistant to Brecht, Carl Weber, drew her attention to it.[73]

In a Brechtian analysis of *Fires*, Carola Hilfrich argues that both Brecht and Smith 'see the theatricality of ordinary eyewitness accounts as crucial to the understanding of the present moment in their culture'.[74] By theatricality, Hilfrich is alluding to two of the processes I named in the Introduction: that actors play roles and that actors perform to live audiences. These are inescapable conditions for providing an eyewitness account, and Smith embraces them both. Teresa Botelho observes that Smith's 'embodiment of the voices she performs creates a distancing effect, where she "is" and simultaneously "is not" the characters she portrays'.[75] Smith's decision to play all her interviewees brings out the role play implicit to both the act of bearing witness and the factors that help determine their social make-up.

The question then arises as to how Smith's approach affects the playtext itself. The monologues are all written in what appears to be verse, but that turns out to be prompts to the performer to signal how each speaker is articulating their ideas, with each line break signifying an element of the respective idea's construction. Some of the scenes also conspicuously reproduce what appear to be the 'ums' of conversational speech. As already noted, Smith connects linguistic rhythms with social identity. As such, these 'ums' are not a mark of naturalistic accuracy, but rather, as Steve Feffer points out, Smith 'listens for

---

[71] Bertolt Brecht, 'The Street Scene', in Brecht, *Brecht on Theatre*, third edition, ed. by Marc Silberman, Steve Giles and Tom Kuhn (London: Bloomsbury, 2014), pp. 176–83 (177).

[72] See, for example, Ange-Marie Hancock, *Intersectionality: An Intellectual History* (New York: Oxford University Press, 2016), pp. 113–4.

[73] See Carl Weber, 'Brecht's "Street Scene" – On Broadway of All Places? A Conversation with Anna Deavere Smith', *Brecht Yearbook*, 20 (1995), pp. 51–63 (53).

[74] Carola Hilfrich, 'Aesthetics of Unease: A Brechtian Study of Anna Deavere Smith's Eyewitness Performance in *Fires in the Mirror*', *Partial Answers*, 7: 2 (2009), pp. 299–318 (301).

[75] Teresa Botelho, 'The Dramatization of Cross-Identity Voicing and the Poetics of Ambiguity', *Hungarian Journal of English and American Studies*, 15: 1 (2009), pp. 79–97 (84).

breaks in language that offset the speaker's dominant patterns'.[76] That is, Smith picks out the points in speech where her interviewees derail their own discourse, unable to pursue a certain ideological train of thought without involuntarily acknowledging it. Overall, the composition of the speeches on the page offers the performer a map through the ideas which, in turn, points to the dynamics of the social role that each interviewee is performing.

An additional dimension arises from metatheatrical self-reference in some of the speeches. In a contextualizing monologue, the physicist Aaron M. Bernstein discusses mirrors, noting that although mirrors are simple objects, they can also distort if they are not constructed properly. Later, Conrad Mohammed, discussing slavery, notes how slavery erased identity, so that the descendants of slaves now bear the names of their oppressors, like Smith and Jones. In these examples, the playtext criticizes itself, as a potentially distorting mirror, and implicates its author as someone not untouched by the broader issues that sparked the riots. Smith acknowledges the precipice she has constructed for herself in order to dispel the notion of objectivity; instead she acknowledges that the playtext, like every playtext, is subject to two inevitable limitations: that it is selective and subjective.

As already mentioned, Smith takes a representative sample of a great many perspectives on the riots and their aftermath. This is not dissimilar to other kinds of verbatim play, such as Gillian Slovo's *The Riots* or Alecky Blythe's *Little Revolution*, both of which deal with the London Riots of 2011. Smith's single-performer approach, however, does something very different from simply aggregating dissenting voices and inviting the audience to reach a judgement. Janelle Reinelt constructs a sophisticated argument to explain Smith's uniqueness. She opens by stating that Smith 'earns the right to speak for others because the performance creates the impression of fidelity and fairness to the interviewees and also because Smith does not disappear into the portraits, thus presuming identification with widely different individuals'. But, she proceeds, this is only a point of departure, a way of validating her decision to play all the figures herself:

> If we agree with Smith that people are not completely trapped by their differences, then this quid pro quo is not enough. It is the bridging of difference which must be enacted, displayed, performed in order to make visible the possibility of replicating it in ordinary life. [...] In a sense, Smith dares to speak for the Hasidim as well as for her own ethnic group not because she is objective, fair minded, and evenhanded, but because she demonstrates

---

[76] Steve Feffer, 'Extending the Breaks: *Fires in the Mirror* in the Context of Hip-Hop Structure, Style, and Culture', *Comparative Drama*, 37: 3&4 (2003–04), pp. 397–415 (408).

the process of bridging difference, seeking information and understanding, and finessing questions of identity.[77]

This is the political function of Smith's extensive role play; she does not simply gather a selection of opposing and contradictory views, something that is certainly a feature of the playtext, but executes a manoeuvre that approaches the difficult prospect of reconciling the different groups represented. The necessity for such a reconciliation is brought out clearly by Gregory Jay, who points to the problems that arise when each ethnic group looks to its own suffering without appreciating a shared legacy: 'These diasporas belong to a common history of Western racism, technological capitalism, and colonial imperialism that encompasses both slavery and the Holocaust.'[78] Smith intentionally highlights each ethnic group's claims to suffering without making Jay's connection as a way of implicitly inviting the audience to do that work.

Both plays discussed in this section engage with the implications of actors playing roles and how that process illuminates the roles people play in everyday life. I deliberately chose these as examples of playtexts in which the figures do not consciously decide to play roles. Instead, they use a curious dramaturgical feature in *Heart's Desire* and the confrontation of carefully ordered authentic material and a single performer, whose onstage identity is always unstable, in *Fires,* to consider how covert role-play can be exposed in the theatre and made subject to scrutiny for its wider social implications.

2 Actors Speak the Words of Others

Look Who's Talking

Actors do not invent their speeches and exchanges; they find them on pages written by other people who sometimes lived millennia before them. Actors accept this as a perfectly normal and reasonable part of their work. But in what ways does this theatrical process reverberate in our real lives? Obviously, we are always speaking other people's words (with the very rare exception of neologisms we may coin) because we did not invent the languages we speak; they pre-exist us, and we learn them through a process of repetition and absorption as we grow up and, with greater maturity, we consult dictionaries and other people to ascertain the meaning of words or phrases we do not understand.

Yet, if these words and linguistic structures come from elsewhere, how do we know that we can rely on them to communicate effectively? After all, it would

---

[77] Janelle Reinelt, 'Performing Race: Anna Deavere Smith's *Fires in the Mirror*', *Modern Drama*, 39 (1996), pp. 609–17 (614 and 615, respectively).

[78] Gregory Jay, 'Other People's Holocausts: Trauma, Empathy, and Justice in Anna Deavere Smith's *Fires in the Mirror*', *Contemporary Literature*, 48: 1 (2007), pp. 119–50 (134).

appear that 'theatricality' originated in the theatre, not in society. It might also appear that certain words' meanings are transparent (although I will call this into question when discussing Peter Handke's *Kaspar*). If I were to say 'I have had that table for two years', the meaning seems clear. However, if I said 'I love you' or 'this is a triumph of justice', the verb 'love' and the noun 'justice' have no clear meaning. What these examples evidence is not only that words precede us, but also that meanings do, too. Obviously, meanings can be contested and we can influence the way that words are used. 'Queer', for instance, was once a term of abuse in the UK, but was reclaimed by the LGBTQ+ community and is now used with pride. All the same, it is rare that an individual speaker determines the common meaning of words; we tend to use them as we find them. As such, our desire to express ourselves is instanced by constructions that exist beyond us, frustrating any simple sense that self-expression is possible.

Jacques Derrida notes that 'the subject [. . .] is inscribed in the language, that he [sic] is a "function" of the language. He becomes a *speaking* subject only by conforming his speech [. . .] to the system of linguistic prescriptions'.[79] The speaker is locked inside this system, with no apparent means to escape it, leading Hans-Georg Gadamer to the counter-intuitive position that 'it is literally more correct to say that language speaks us, rather than that we speak it'.[80] Here he suggests that while we select our words, the choice is radically limited and overdetermined. That is, we have to order our words in such a way that they make sense, deferring our choices to a system of grammar and syntax, and the words themselves will be subject to conventions regarding their usage. So, we hold a meeting, but we do not carry one; we smell a rat, not a mouse; we identify a dead, not a deceased metaphor. Language is continually telling us what to do, not vice versa.

This inversion of common sense regarding our relationship to language upsets certain ideas about personhood and our ability to communicate. Language does not serve our ends, rather, we serve its. However, the more disturbing corollary of this discovery is that language also opens us up to the wills and desires of more powerful and potentially pernicious interests because it is ideologically inflected. Joachim Fiebach notes that 'Althusser argued that ideology has a "material existence". Inscribed in practical social actions, it determines them. This is true not only for the activities of the ideological institutions (State, Church, the Educational System) but for the individual as

---

[79] Jacques Derrida, 'Differance', in Derrida, *Speech and Phenomena and other Essays on Husserl's Theory of Signs*, tr. by David B. Allison (Evanston: Northwestern University Press, 1973), pp. 129–60 (145–6).

[80] Hans-Georg Gadamer, *Truth and Method*, second edition, tr. by Joel Weinsheimer and Donald G. Marshall (New York: Crossroad, 1989), p. 463.

well.'[81] Let us briefly consider two different ways of approaching ideology, which, I concede, simplifies the term. On the one hand, we might consider ideology as a kind of social glue; it is the stuff that holds societies together. This might be a positive thing in that we respect other people's personal space in the street, but it has shadier connotations when, say, walking past a homeless person on that street gives one no undue cause for concern. Here ideology tends to affect our value and behavioural systems unconsciously. We do not have to question every aspect of our daily lives because a set of prepared responses is already present. On the other hand, ideology can function as social dynamite. When we observe the world and seek to change it, we develop ideas consciously and seek to implement them. The plight of the poor in the early twentieth century led to revolution in Russia and the establishment of the welfare state in the UK. In both instances, ideas about the poor created new realities.

Language is one of the ways that we negotiate social reality by describing and interacting with it. But if the language we use is suffused with ideological meanings that we do not control, we find ourselves conforming to values that may not represent our best interests. On 24 February 2022, Russians learned that a 'special military operation' was underway in Ukraine; NATO declared this an 'invasion' and a 'war'. One's choice of term will reflect an ideological position towards the same events, yet sometimes choice is curtailed, in public at least, when, here, the Russian Federation banned the use of the words 'war', 'attack' and 'invasion' with respect to Ukraine in the media.[82]

Theatre has become suspicious of attempts to naturalize language. Perhaps one of the first instances of calling this into question was implemented by Brecht. He criticized the notion of originality in an essay on plagiarism and art, written in 1929, and wrote: 'Here is where quotation finds its naturally significant place. It is thus the most important stylistic device: quotability.'[83] Brecht suggests that quoting material is more important than suggesting novelty or originality, something that language, as discussed above, only appears to offer. He turned these insights into rehearsal practice in a better-known essay, written a decade or so later, in which he invited his actors to rehearse their lines in the third person and in the past.[84] As such, the Brechtian actor was

---

[81] Joachim Fiebach, 'Theatricality: From Oral Traditions to Televised "Realities"', *SubStance*, 31: 2&3 (2002), pp. 17–41 (22).

[82] See, for example, Andrew Roth, '"Don't Call It a War" – Propaganda Filters the Truth about Ukraine on Russian Media', *The Guardian*, 26 February 2022. www.theguardian.com/world/2022/feb/26/propaganda-filters-truth-ukraine-war-russian-media [accessed on 12 March 2024].

[83] Bertolt Brecht, '[Plagiat und Kunst]', in Brecht, *Große kommentierte Berliner und Frankfurter Ausgabe*, Werner Hecht, Jan Knopf, Werner Mittenzwei and Klaus-Detlef Müller, (eds.), Vol. 21 (Berlin: Aufbau, 1992), p. 318. All translations from the German are mine.

[84] Bertolt Brecht, 'Short Description of a New Technique of Acting that Produces a *Verfremdung* Effect', in Brecht, *Brecht on Theatre*, pp. 184–96 (186).

encouraged to present text in inverted commas, as if someone else had spoken it elsewhere. The effect is to draw attention to the lack of originality of the speeches in the hope that the audience might question where the language has come from and whose interests it serves.

In the plays examined below, I will be focussing on the interplay of language and ideology, and how the proposition that we, like actors, speak the words of others affects the subject.

Peter Handke, *Kaspar*

To my knowledge, *Kaspar* (premiere 1968) is the only play that deals with language acquisition in a systematic way. It takes its lead from a real event when a youth called Kaspar Hauser appeared on a street in Nuremberg in 1828, apparently without the capacity to speak and equipped only with a single sentence. Once he had learned to speak, he said that he had spent his childhood isolated in a dark room. Handke takes this condition, abstracting and generalizing it, as he states in a note to the work: 'The play *Kaspar* does not show how IT REALLY IS or REALLY WAS with Kaspar Hauser. It shows what IS POSSIBLE with someone'.[85] Kaspar becomes a model of a human being who is taught how to speak over the course of sixty-five scenes. Throughout the play, Kaspar can be seen on stage, while disembodied voices teach him language. The voices are provided by a neologism of Handke's own, 'Einsager'. While the official translation calls them prompters, Bettina L. Kapp prefers 'indoctrinators'.[86] Unfortunately, neither version quite does justice to Handke. 'Prompters' is a little too passive, as if Kaspar had forgotten his words and needed a reminder; 'indoctrinators' is a little too aggressive, even though, as I will demonstrate, that this is precisely what they are doing. Literally, these are speakers who get inside one's head, but as no word exists for this in English, I will retain the official translation's rendition, thereby acknowledging my own inability to fashion a new term.

Handke tells us that the prompters' voices should be 'completely comprehensible, their manner of speaking should be that of voices which in reality have a technical medium interposed between themselves and the listeners'.[87] That is, the voices should not be coloured, lending them a veneer of neutrality; yet they are not in Kaspar's space, they have to be piped into it. They could thus exist as

---

[85] Peter Handke, 'Introduction', tr. by Michael Roloff, in Handke, *Plays*, volume 1 (London: Methuen, 1997), pp. 53–5 (53).

[86] Bettina L. Knapp, 'Peter Handke's *Kaspar*: The Mechanics of Language – A Fractionating Schizophrenic Theatrical Event', *Studies in 20th Century Literature*, 14: 2 (1990), pp. 241–59 (249).

[87] Handke, 'Introduction', p. 53.

recordings, a standard programme for all. As Handke makes clear later in the playtext: '*Over a good amplifying system they speak a text that is not theirs.*'[88] The play opens, emphasizing that the audience is in a theatre. Handke states that the objects on stage 'look theatrical: not because they imitate other objects, but because the way they are situated with respect to one another does not correspond to their usual arrangement in reality'.[89] So, when Kaspar arranges them later, they will lose their theatricality and will appear to be in some way natural. The play thus dramatizes the process of naturalization, something it will continue to do with respect to language. Kaspar himself is also presented as unnatural; he wears a mask of astonishment. The world he encounters is strange and he tries to deploy the one sentence he has to make sense of it.

The prompters' voices are then heard, and they force Kaspar to lose his sentence. They systematically dismantle it with their own linguistic assault. They associate ignorance with pain: 'The shoelace hurts you. It does not hurt you because it is a shoelace but because you lack the word for it' (66). As Linda Hill observes, 'Violence and order, which are opposites according to common sense, are declared interdependent since violence establishes order'.[90] And order is the order of the day in *Kaspar*, as the prompters state, 'Every object must be a picture of an object [. . .]. Every proper table [. . .] is orderly, pretty, comfortable, peaceful, inconspicuous, useful, in good taste' (77). A table is thus not a table when it is dirty or has fallen over. Indeed, in plain English, if we saw a table that had fallen over, we would not describe the room as simply containing a table; we would qualify its state. The prompters thus reveal the ideological underpinning of even the most apparently transparent meanings of words.

From the imposition of ideological value to inanimate objects, the prompters dictate a long series of maxims to Kaspar while he makes the stage orderly and less 'theatrical', as Handke called it earlier. These include: 'Everyone is born with a wealth of talents / Everyone is responsible for his own progress / Everything that does harm is made harmless' (79). Perhaps one of the most disturbing features of the lines is their universality; there are no exceptions to some frankly questionable positions. Hills notes: 'The prompters speeches are an anthology of non-sequiturs based on fiat, association and shift in meanings'.[91]

---

[88] Peter Handke, *Kaspar*, tr. by Michael Roloff, in Handke, *Plays*, volume 1 (London: Methuen, 1997), pp. 51–141 (60). Subsequent references to the playtext will appear as bracketed page numbers in the main text.
[89] Handke, 'Introduction', p. 54.
[90] Linda Hill, 'Obscurantism and Verbal Resistance in Handke's *Kaspar*', *The Germanic Review*, 52: 4 (1977), pp. 304–15 (305).
[91] Ibid., p. 306.

Having been primed for linguistic programming, the prompters declare, 'You have been cracked open' (101). In twelve subsequent scenes, the process of universalization is reconfigured as Kaspar is joined on stage by identical Kaspars who illustrate a certain proposition. So, when the prompters announce, 'You become sensitive to dirt' (102), another Kaspar enters and sweeps the dirt around the first Kaspar, who is sitting in a rocking chair. By the end of the first part, Kaspar has become a model of orderly domesticity. After he leaves the stage, the doors of the onstage wardrobe slowly open. He cannot control his world fully.

Scene 59 is the intermission. And while the spectators relax outside the auditorium, they hear real taped speeches made by all manner of public figures, but none of the sentences is complete. Here, Handke translates the theatricality on stage into the spectators' real world. The second-hand language of the entire playtext is reproduced as a series of real examples, directly relating the stage world to the audience's own experiences.

The shorter, second part commences with all seven Kaspars on stage, now wearing masks of contentment. Scene 62 opens with an unsettling stage direction: '*Kaspar, at the microphone, begins to speak. His voice begins to resemble the voices of the prompters*' (120–1). Two scenes later he acknowledges, 'Already with my first sentence I was trapped' (138). Yet, as he is speaking, the other Kaspars start to file away at the objects on stage that had been arranged so neatly. In the final scene, the Kaspars destroy the set, and the first Kaspar reveals a file of his own with which he attacks the microphone into which he had previously been speaking. He causes the theatre's curtains to close by reciting the formula 'Goats and monkeys' in ever higher tones until they finally close, toppling all the Kaspars over behind the curtain.

'Goats and monkeys' may sound like an odd combination of words, yet they are actually a line from Shakespeare's *Othello*. The apparently nonsensical use of language, a potential exit from the world of order, is itself a quotation. Indeed, earlier in the play, other odd formulations, such as 'Why are there so many black worms flying about?' (100), are also literary quotations (here from Horváth's play *Faith, Hope and Charity*). Literature is revealed as a qualified route out of the prison house of language. June Schlueter considers how apt the Othello comparison is: 'for who more than the Moor of Venice succeeds so perfectly in ordering his world, in controlling his reality through language?'.[92] She continues to show how both Othello and Kaspar lose control of language and their situation.

---

[92] June Schlueter, '"Goats and Monkeys" and the "Idiocy of Language": Handke's *Kaspar* and Shakespeare's *Othello*', *Modern Drama*, 23: 1 (1980), pp. 25–32 (27).

Kaspar's language acquisition is predicated on a system of order, but it is worth identifying the role of order in the greater social framework. Critics have been somewhat coy about this issue. M. Read suggests that the prompters 'epitomise the world of rational discourse and the purely functional use of language',[93] and Ulf Olsson notes that the politics of the play is less important than the way that the prompters' words 'express a view on the world as form-[ing] part of the training and disciplining of Kaspar'.[94] These conclusions prioritize a formal procedure of language learning over the ideological values that self-same training instil, but I contend that the two cannot be treated discretely; they are inseparable. Here, a specifically German word association helps. While 'order' in English may indeed represent a general state of things functioning 'as they should', in German the word is closely associated with the rise of the bourgeoisie.[95] Here, order represents the values of this middle class and their imposition in this play represents disaster.

As Robert Stockheimer notes, Kaspar himself is not an empty vessel for the prompters' words; he 'is not just driven to parrot prevailing opinions'.[96] This independently minded figure thus demonstrates the difficulties and dangers involved when we speak the words of others. These words contain numerous ideological positions that nonetheless manifest themselves physically in the pain Kaspar feels. Yet this pain is not an abstract or general symptom; it is intimately connected to the values present in the new language Kaspar is forced to acquire. As such, the playtext demonstrates both the palpable benefits that language confers, but, perhaps more crucially, the remarkable costs. It does this by exposing the processes involved and their attendant debt to ideological content.

Caryl Churchill, *Blue Kettle*

Blue Kettle (premiere 1997) is the companion piece to *Heart's Desire*, the playtext discussed in the previous section. Both were performed under the title *Blue Heart*. The two plays were not written for this purpose, but director Max Stafford-Clark and Churchill agreed that they actually complemented each

---

[93] M. Read, 'Peter Handke's *Kaspar* and the Power of Negative Thinking', *Forum for Modern Language Studies*, 24: 2 (1993), pp.126–48 (133).

[94] Ulf Olsson, *Silence and Subject in Modern Literature. Spoken Violence* (Basingstoke: Palgrave, 2013), p. 158.

[95] See, for example, Eckart Conze, 'Eine bürgerliche Republik? Bürgertum und Bürgerlichkeit in der westdeutschen Nachkriegsgesellschaft', *Geschichte und Gesellschaft*, 30: 3 (2004), pp. 527–42.

[96] Robert Stockhammer, 'We Shall Therefore Never Write about What Took Place or Did Not Take Place in May', *Interventions*, 23: 3 (2021), pp. 448–62 (454).

other.[97] Ostensibly, this is a difficult link to make, given that their forms are so radically different. *Blue Kettle* is about a confidence artist, Derek, who seeks out elderly women who gave up their sons for adoption, pretending to be that son for each mother.

The first scene between Derek and Mrs Plant looks like the start of a standard realist playtext: there is an exchange in unstylized language. Derek has just revealed himself to be her long-lost son, as her first line, 'I can't speak,' registers her surprise.[98] However, as will emerge quickly, this opening line resonates throughout the rest of the playtext. That is because the words 'blue' and 'kettle' start to replace random words in the ten subsequent scenes. Initially, there is one 'blue', spoken by Derek, and one 'kettle' by his next 'mother', Mrs Oliver, in scene two, suggesting perhaps a gendered binary of distribution, but this interpretation falls apart as the 'blue's and 'kettle's proliferate to such an extent that by the final scene, only the first line contains the words 'blue' and 'kettle' before the words, more often than not, appear as fragments of themselves or only as single letters. And although 'blue' is an adjective and 'kettle' is a noun, when substituted for other words, they change into other parts of speech, too, as when Derek asks Mrs Plant: 'So blue didn't anyone let you know?' (105) where 'blue' stands in for the interrogative pronoun 'why'.

Churchill suggests that the double-bill 'can be roughly linked in subject matter by being described as a family waiting for their daughter and a son looking for his mother. But the plays are McGuffins – my main intention was their destruction'.[99] However, in the context of the theatrical processes I am examining to understand the nature of theatricality, both playtexts explore the proposition that actors play roles and that actors speak the words of other people. And it is here that I will be exploring the second process in greater detail.

Unlike in *Kaspar*, attention is not at first drawn to the fact that the play's figures are speaking other people's words, instead, this emerges over time. So, in the first scene, an entirely conventional dramatic dialogue appears to be unfolding. It is only in the second scene that the reader notes that Derek is playing out the same scenario, but with a different adoptive mother. As the play continues, we meet two further adoptive mothers, Mrs Vane and Miss Clarence. The situation is thus always the same: Derek is using language to convince the

---

[97] See Elaine Aston, *Caryl Churchill*, second edition (Tavistock: Northcote House, 2001), p. 113.

[98] Caryl Churchill, *Blue Kettle*, in Churchill, *Plays*, volume 4 (London: Nick Hern, 2008), pp. 97–128 (99). Subsequent references to the playtext will appear as bracketed page numbers in the main text.

[99] Churchill, 'Introduction', in Churchill, *Plays*, volume 4 (London: Nick Hern, 2008), pp. vii–x (viii).

elderly women of his identity, as he has no biological or biographical data to offer. As such, he is tapping into the language of sincerity, and what we read is a series of permutations. In one scene, the mother saw a family resemblance, in the next she did not; in one the father is dead and did not know about the adoption, in another the opposite is true. In all the permutations, however, Derek is successful in establishing his place in their families as their long-lost son. None of the mothers query his story because the language he accesses is deployed so successfully.

This is emphasized in scene seven when Derek and his girlfriend Enid have a meal at Mrs Vane's, with her husband present, too. Mrs Vane announces that Derek is the son she gave away and Mr. Vane is very positive about the surprising news. Enid then makes the shocking claim that Derek is a fraud. Yet he counters by accusing Enid of being jealous of his new mother's love for him. Enid's final appeal to the Vanes is: 'Believe me' (118). But belief is Derek's currency and it is not devalued easily. What becomes evident over the course of these scenes is the constant repetition of linguistic patterns, an unmissable feature of *Heart's Desire*, too, and this draws attention to the way in which his language performs the act of persuasion.

However, Derek tests his ruses to destruction towards the end of the play. In the penultimate scene, he engineers an encounter between two of his adoptive mothers, a situation that can only lead to disaster for at least one of the women. Initially, Mrs Oliver's 'revelation' that she is Derek's mother leads to further confusion, in that Mrs Plant believes that Mrs Oliver adopted Derek while Mrs Plant was his biological mother. But by the end of the scene, both mothers claim that they are the biological mothers because Derek sought them both. Derek says that there must have been a problem in the 'documentation' (126), taking recourse to evidence that exists outside his linguistic stratagems, although he does not have it with him.

Derek's duplicity towards the elderly women is not the only deception in the play. Mrs Vane pretends that she met Derek while volunteering at a local hospital; Enid invents a cousin for her dead aunt's husband. And in the final scene, Derek appears to tell Mrs Plant the true story of his search for adoptive mothers. Yet he still lies, telling her that his mother died when he was a child (although we learned that she was alive, but unwell, in scene eight), thus casting doubt on the sincerity of the 'true' story he was telling. Language becomes a means for constructing worlds, something already instanced in all its contradictions in *Kaspar*. The problem is that meaning is not inevitably linked to its referents because that relationship, as Saussure identified, is arbitrary. Here, the increasing repetition of 'blue' and 'kettle' intensifies the fact.

For the whole play, it is not clear why Derek is acting as he does. In scene nine, Enid asks whether it is fraud or a psychological 'hangup' (120). He finally says, 'It is both it is neither' (121); the text offers nothing more than that, which is not necessarily unsatisfactory; the play is far more concerned with the way that language is being used rather than why. And this accounts for the ever-burgeoning substitutions of 'blue' and 'kettle' over the course of the scenes.

The presence of the two words is obviously unusual. The play's title already shows that their first fleeting inclusion is no typo, and as their number proliferates, it is impossible to ignore them. One is provoked to investigate their function. Critics have, of course, been fascinated by the ways these foreign words invade and undermine coherence in the playtext. Rabascall notes, 'Such unintelligibility will turn into a complete disestablishment of the codes that govern language to such an extent that, by the end of the piece, we will witness its disappearance.'[100] Elaine Aston concurs, 'Language, through which we communicate and make sense of the world, is increasingly damaged, deformed in conjunction with the intensifying complex play of fictional, familial identities.'[101] Jernigan, extending the textual difficulties to their performance, opines, 'perhaps, the actors themselves are machines and are suffering through a [. . .] software glitch.'[102] But what these interpretations miss is that in performance, the director and the actors have to agree on what the implied or possible meanings of any line may be. Often there is clear linguistic context, as when Mrs Plant says, 'It's the tip of a kettle' (123) where 'kettle' stands for the dead metaphor 'iceberg'. Elsewhere meaning is totally unknowable, as when Enid says, 'Blue blue blue blue blue today in the street, I begged' (121). Here the actors, in concert with the director, have to agree on a meaning for the scene to progress. Gobert addresses this issue:

> Critics have connected the faltering language of *Blue Kettle* to the disintegration of identity as Derek's ploy gradually fails. But this misreading projects the audience's own disconnection from the stage back onto its characters. Note the precision with which [scene ten] moves closer to greater clarity in spite of the linguistic play.[103]

That is, the figures understand each other perfectly, something made even more apparent in the final scene where any clear sense of what is actually being said is obliterated by the fragmentary deployment of 'blue' and 'kettle'. This scene in particular highlights a fascinating collision of the artificial and the sincere. The figures on stage are clearly speaking nonsense, yet, in their roles, they seem to

[100] Rabascall, *Gender, Politics, Subjectivity*, p. 275.   [101] Aston, *Caryl Churchill*, p. 115.
[102] Jernigan, *'Traps, Softcops, Blue Heart* and *This Is a Chair'*, p. 24.
[103] Gobert, 'On Performance and Selfhood in Caryl Churchill', p. 117.

be looking for genuine connection (see Postlewaite and Davis's proposition on p. 15). So, while readers may well be frustrated, spectators can watch scenes play out with actors addressing each other as if the words 'blue' and 'kettle' had transparent meanings. And it is here that the playtext highlights the process that actors speak the words of other people.

The actors can deduce or interpret the meanings of two semantically non-sensical words, words that are clearly not their charaters' own choice of words. The *system of language* allows them to establish meaning through, here, clear expression rather than the usual meanings attached to the words 'blue' and 'kettle'. Grammar and syntax determine meaning in these instances, regardless of precisely which words are being used; language is speaking us. In *Blue Kettle,* this idea is taken to an extreme.

Yet, whereas in *Kaspar*, the ideology of bourgeois order informed the values of the prompters' language, in this play, the ideology of feelings and familial bonds is subject to scrutiny. Derek is able to play the role of the lost son by selecting the appropriate linguistic designations to engineer relationships where they do not exist. He speaks the words of other people to achieve his dubious ends, playing on social values that pervade the words. When, for example, he asks Miss Clarence, 'Do you mind if I ask who my father was?' (114), the line represents far more than a simple question. It opens with three polite words, establishing Derek's humility, even though he knows that the man in question was not his father. Derek also maintains a respectful distance by using 'father' rather than a more familiar 'dad' and omitting 'you' after 'ask'. He carefully negotiates the ideological underpinnings of the social situation and achieves his ends.

What both *Kaspar* and *Blue Kettle* show is that individuals neither control nor shape language; it functions outside them and they have to choose according to *its* rules. Its lack of concrete reference to the world means that it is always liable to abuse. On the one hand, both plays show what happens when language is wielded by the powerful in the form of the prompters and Derek. On the other hand, power is never the guarantor of mastery. Kaspar rejects the language he has been taught, commanding the curtains with a single, seemingly nonsensical but intertextual phrase, whose pitch when being delivered seems to be doing the work. Derek finds himself adrift: the coterie of adoptive mothers does not satisfy him, and all he is left with is a world of lies.

It is difficult to derive a clear stance towards language from the plays. Rather, what emerges is a necessary scepticism and the need for vigilance. Language pre-exists all its speakers, and it comes with often covert ideological baggage because it pretends to offer unmediated access to a world of things and ideas. Both plays show people speaking the words of others. *Kaspar* does this systematically, enacting a process of language learning and, ultimately, language rejection. *Blue Kettle* uses the everyday language of interpersonal relationships and takes two different approaches to it in order to expose its artifice. It presents repeated permutations of the same situation, establishing that similar formulations of language can be used to negotiate them. It then makes a radical intervention by replacing words we would recognize with two that do not belong there. Language, as the playtexts amply demonstrate, is all we have to communicate the complexities (and the simplicities) of the world, but it is speaking us, not vice versa, and so both plays give their readers and spectators troubling grounds for wariness.

3 Actors Are Given Instructions by Others

Instructions Provided

Today, directors, usually the most important people to give instructions to actors, are often considered an essential part of the staging process. Their *modus operandi* is flexible and can include providing an overall vision for a production, specific approaches to acting and delivering the playtext, often by engaging the actors in the creative process as creative partners. But directors can also grant actors greater degrees of freedom at times. For example, Sarah Kane's *4:48 Psychosis* includes no character attribution; there are no named roles, just text to be delivered. When it was performed by students at the Central School of Speech and Drama in London in November 2003, all performers had to learn the entire playtext.[104] They then had the opportunity to deliver whichever lines they wanted, either solo or as a chorus, as the performance dynamic took them every night, acting, of course, within a set of parameters rehearsed with the director. A similar approach was taken to Heiner Müller's experimental play, *The Hamletmaschine*, in 1984.[105] Directors can thus have a major role in shaping a production or grant actors greater creative freedom while nonetheless determining the aesthetic frame.

As already noted in the Introduction, giving instructions to actors clearly existed in one form or another throughout theatre history. Hamlet, for example, famously gives direction to the travelling players in III ii. And in certain ancient Greek tragedies, three actors played the main roles, suggesting the need for differentiation, both vocally and physically, and in terms of different masks worn throughout the performance. Indeed, Marianne McDonald speculates that 'Sophocles' weak voice prevented him from acting in his own plays. He

---

[104] The information was provided to me by the director, Geoff Colman.

[105] See Eva Elisabeth Brenner, '*Hamletmachine*' *Onstage: A Critical Analysis of Heiner Müller's Play in Production* (PhD thesis: New York University, 1994), pp. 337 and 351.

probably remained as director'.[106] It is, in other words, hard to conceive of a theatrical production that does not include some kind of direction. It might be overt or based more on an implicit theatrical tradition, but, either way, there is no sense that actors enter the stage without a clear sense of what they are about to do.

The modulation between distinct and evident direction, and more covert or subtle instruction, also finds its place in our experience of everyday life. The law, for example, lays down the rules for behaviour, from obvious prohibitions of killing other people to the finer details about how one is to conduct oneself in public. But there is a great range of other behaviours to which one is expected to conform that are not officially codified. Staring at people one encounters in the street is considered ill-mannered in some cultures; violating people's personal space and speaking too loudly in public spaces like restaurants or theatres are similarly frowned upon at certain times and in certain places. But it is worth noting these cultural specificities as, for example, shouting at the stage during a British pantomime is actively encouraged while doing this during other kinds of production would not be acceptable. Behaving as one does in one's own country may well be thrown into sharp relief when abroad, that is, when one has not yet received the relevant instructions.

More often than not, instructions are not given overtly. Instead, they permeate behaviour we observe or representations of behaviour in various media. Judith Butler has explored gender as a performance and argues that it is 'an identity instituted through a *stylized repetition of acts*'. She observes that 'to be female is [...] to induce the body to become a cultural sign, to materialize oneself in obedience to an historically delimited possibility'.[107] The notion of 'obedience' is important here, in that one is encouraged to conform to a set of strictures that may appear in law (women not having the right to vote or own property), but are more often communicated culturally in a set of behaviours or representations that are either condoned or condemned. Consider reactions to men growing their hair long in the late 1960s, the reception of Boy George's gender-bending appearance in the early 1980s, or responses to the trans community today. The instructions for how to behave in any given time or space are often implicit and unspoken, yet transgressing them exposes their basis and can lead to all manner of sanction. That instructions are policed will be considered in the next section.

---

[106] Marianne McDonald, *The Living Art of Greek Tragedy* (Bloomington: Indiana University Press, 2003), p. 3.

[107] Judith Butler, 'Performative Acts and Gender Constitution: An Essay in Phenomenology and Feminist Theory', *Theatre Journal*, 40: 4 (1988), pp. 519–31 (both 519 and 522, respectively).

The idea of instruction in everyday life is extensive and comprehensive. Almost every aspect of our social lives is determined and then regulated in some way or another, and so the overt process that actors are given instructions by others can be detected in the more covert processes that exist beyond the stage. And while the identities of the actors in the outside world are obvious – we are all the actors – those of the 'others' are sometimes inscrutable. Who, for instance, says that men should behave in a certain way and women in another? Who says that we should follow our self-interest, and who says that we should help our fellow citizens? Directing people's behaviours is evidently based on a power relationship, and by detecting instruction in playtexts, we can start to investigate the nature of these relationships and speculate on the nature of the dynamic. And if we can identify the ways in which it functions, we might be able to change it if we find it oppressive. The two playtexts chosen for analysis explore the relationship between instructor and instructed in both the formal arrangement of a rehearsal in the theatre and the context of instructions being issued in everyday life.

Samuel Beckett, *Catastrophe*

Although Beckett frequently referenced the theatre in his plays,[108] none of them is explicitly set in a theatre, with the exception of *Catastrophe* (premiere 1982). This short piece was commissioned by the Association Internationale de Défense des Artistes for a special night of work devoted to Václav Havel. At that time, he was an imprisoned playwright, but later became President of Czechoslovakia and then the Czech Republic. Beckett dedicated the play to him. In it, a male director (abbreviated by Beckett to D), supported by his female assistant (A), gets an actor (referred to as the Protagonist, P) to perform a demeaning role to depict the abstract term 'catastrophe'. At the end of the rehearsal, P is carefully posed so that he does not look at the audience, an effect that D says will 'have them on their feet'. And indeed it does: mysteriously, the rehearsal becomes the performance and we hear the *'distant storm of applause'*.[109] Yet at that moment, P raises his head, against D's express instructions, and the applause dissipates. There is a long pause before the only light, the one on P's face, fades out.

---

[108] See, for example, Juana Christina von Stein, 'The Theater of the Absurd and the Absurdity of Theater: The Early Plays of Beckett and Ionesco', in Elena Penskaya and Joachim Küpper (eds.), *Theater as Metaphor* (Berlin: De Gruyter, 2019), pp. 217–37.

[109] Samuel Beckett, *Catastrophe*, in Beckett, *The Complete Dramatic Works* (London: Faber & Faber, 1986), pp. 455–61 (both quotations 461). Subsequent references to the playtext will appear as bracketed page numbers in the main text.

Curiously, *Catastrophe* has been called 'realistic' at times,[110] but this is a peculiar characterization. D is set up as a caricature from the off, dressed in a fur coat with matching headwear. The dialogue is clipped and impersonal, as Bert O. States notes, the language 'implies the security of class membership. To say [as D does] "Lovely" or "Terrific!" (at least here) is to be in possession of your world'.[111] But D's language, as Trish McTighe notes, is alien to the actual workings of the theatre. D 'is unable to make himself understood by the lighting technician' and A has to tell the technician what to do.[112] So, his language is limited and he cannot exercise control universally, even in the space he believed was his own. It is also impossible to ignore the way that A repeats the response to D's instructions 'I make a note' (458) eight times, which is hardly an example of realistic speech.

There is also little sense that this *is* a real rehearsal. According to the stage directions, what we see are the '*final touches to the last scene*' (457), but D asks a series of questions to which he should certainly know the answer ('Why the hat'? [. . .] 'Why the gown?' (ibid.)), which States calls 'catechistic'.[113] That is, the language is not natural, but follows a predetermined pattern; he is speaking the words of others. When understood like that, D is testing A and ensuring that she responds correctly to his questions, which establishes an additional coordinate of his power. The silence of P and the magical transformation from rehearsal to performance also act to undermine any sense of mimetic realism. I thus suggest that the play is not a realistic depiction of a rehearsal, but a model of a process. A model is not concerned with the specifics of a particular time or place, but rather with relationships and their exemplary configuration. What, then, is being modelled?

Clearly, D is at the centre of the action; he drives the play and engineers what seems to be his artistic triumph. He is fastidious, directing with great precision to achieve his effects.[114] But he is also plugged into a larger system. At one point, he commands, 'Step on it, I have a caucus' (458). While the use of the

---

[110] David Warrilow, who acted in the US premiere, noted the 'real psychology' in D, quoted in Jonathan Kalb, *Beckett in Performance* (Cambridge: Cambridge University Press, 1989), p. 224; and Nick Wolterman suggests that the play 'stages a relatively realistic situation that might seem out of place alongside more enigmatic or introspective dramatic works of the late 1970s and early 1980s', in 'Playing the Crowd: Beckett, Havel, and Their Audiences', *Textual Practice*, 34: 4 (2020), pp. 691–712 (693).

[111] Bert O. States, '*Catastrophe*: Beckett's Laboratory/Theatre', *Modern Drama*, 30: 1 (1987), pp. 14–22 (15).

[112] Trish McTighe, 'Everyday Catastrophes: Gender, Labour and Power in Beckett's Theatre. Structural Maintenance', *Journal of Beckett Studies*, 28: 1 (2019), pp. 19–34 (24).

[113] Ibid., p. 17.

[114] Several critics have made the metatheatrical connection between D and Beckett's own practices as a theatre director. See, for example, Laura Peja, 'Victimised Actors and Despotic Directors: Clichés of Theatre at Stake in Beckett's *Catastrophe*', in S. E. Gontarski (ed.), *The Edinburgh*

word 'caucus' instead of the more usual 'meeting' already signals that he is speaking someone else's words for self-aggrandizement, his role there remains elusive. Is he hurrying there to chair the session, or does he need to attend so as not to miss out? Whatever the answer is, his place there contributes to his importance, and so there is a connection between his behaviour in the rehearsal room and his place outside it. The catechistic exchanges with A confirm the power hierarchy as she continually submits to her superior. She appears to perform her own act of resistance when she sits in D's chair, but immediately *'wipes vigorously back and seat of chair, discards rag, sits again'* (459). McTighe notes: 'While her gesture might be seen as revolt, it is not really consequential to the outcome of the scene.'[115] As such, the showy removal of D's sweat does little to alter A's place in the power relation – her ostentatious disgust remains an empty gesture.

As Wolterman notes, 'Reportedly, for Beckett, P's final gesture was an unambiguous gesture of protest: "He's saying, you bastards, you haven't fin-ished me yet".'[116] The idea that P is involved in an 'act of defiance'[117] is unmistakable. Up until now, P, an ironic epithet if ever there was one,[118] has silently accepted the humiliations heaped on him by D. P resists D's instructions and at this moment, as Angela Moorjani notes, 'the Protagonist becomes his own director'.[119]

But rather than interpreting the final act as one of defiance, I prefer to follow Antoni Libera in his description of 'the Protagonist's refusal to conform to [D's] will by means of a gesture which has been clearly and explicitly rejected, or even prohibited, by [D]'.[120] In terms of the play as a model, a failure to conform acknowledges that a direction has not been obeyed, but does not dwell on the possible reasons for this. The result, however, is clear. The audience, enraptured by D's depiction of catastrophe, withdraws their applause when the object of their gaze looks back at them. The refusal to carry out the instructions leads to a catastrophe for the performance.

But there is more to the failure to conform than simply leaving the stage audience cold. As Anna McMullan shows, following Foucault's *Discipline and Punish*, Beckett establishes a connection between looking and the stage as a disciplinary space. She notes that the first action of the play is '*D and*

Companion to Samuel Beckett and the Arts (Edinburgh: Edinburgh University Press, 2014), pp. 386–96 (387).

115 McTighe, 'Everyday Catastrophes', p. 27.   116 Wolterman, 'Playing the Crowd', p. 698.

117 Kalb, *Beckett in Performance*, p. 16.

118 See Laura Peja, 'Victimised Actors and Despotic Directors', pp. 388–9.

119 Angela Moorjani, 'Directing or In-Directing Beckett: Or What Is Wrong with *Catastrophe*'s Director?', *Samuel Beckett Today*, 15 (2005), pp.187–99 (196).

120 Antoni Libera, 'Beckett's *Catastrophe*', *Modern Drama*, 28: 3 (1985), pp. 341–47 (342).

A *contemplate* P' (457).[121] By its end, however, something peculiar happens to us, the spectators. States observes how cleverly Beckett positions the stage audience and the real audience, the stage director and the real director.[122] That is, the real audience hears how the stage audience applauds the inhumane work of D, yet at the end of the show, it asks itself whether or not it should be applauding the work of the real director who staged *Catastrophe*. Jim Hansen, who reads the play as an eloquent critique of audience sympathy and identification with P, understands that an interesting inversion has taken place: 'Let me pose the actual problem of *Catastrophe*'s conclusion in a different, but perhaps more direct, way: I do not bear witness to P's shame so much as P bears witness to mine.'[123] He sees the doubling of audiences and directors as a way of indicting the audience (something to which I will return in the next section).

The play, when considered as a model, reveals the complex relationships between cause and effect. We observe an authoritarian yet meticulous director dispensing instructions, aided and abetted by A, and followed precisely yet silently by P. The lighting technician, not of D's class, cannot, however, understand him and requires a 'translation' provided by A, something that marks a first limit to D's power. Performance itself marks the second, when P finally realizes his own agency. His intervention destroys D's carefully crafted effect and opens up new possibilities, founded solely on the refusal to conform to instruction. The metatheatrical pivot shifts an audience experiencing another audience to an audience finding itself being posed a question in its own world. Does it obey the convention, which is itself a covert instruction, and applaud, or does it, like P, refuse? Beckett's dramaturgical mechanism manages to present us with a model of relationships in an imagined theatre and then transforms them into the workings of a real theatre in which the ethical issues, writ large in the playtext, still obtain.

Bertolt Brecht, *The Decision*

The Decision (also translated as *The Measures Taken*, premiered in 1930) apparently does not take place in a theatre, but in and around a very fictional China, where a successful left-wing revolution has been instigated by a mere four Agitators. They return from their mission to report that in the course of their work, they had to kill one of their number, the Young Comrade. This has led to a number of commentators, including Theodor Adorno, to condemn the play for

---

[121] Anna McMullan, *Theatre on Trial. Samuel Beckett's Later Drama* (London: Routledge, 1993), p. 27.

[122] See States, '*Catastrophe*: Beckett's Laboratory/Theatre', p. 20.

[123] Jim Hansen, 'Samuel Beckett's *Catastrophe* and the Theater of Pure Means', *Contemporary Literature*, 49: 4 (2008), pp. 660–82 (668–9).

its apparent justification of Stalinist purges.[124] However, the dramaturgy of the play actually points to a different interpretation entirely.

The Agitators retell, in flashback, to a Control Chorus (a mass representation of a Communist Party), the key incidents that led up to the killing, and the Agitators all play the Young Comrade in the different episodes, as well as a host of other figures. As such, *The Decision* does actually take place in a theatre as the actors continue to swap parts. Indeed, the play is one of Brecht's *Lehrstücke*, a 'learning play'. The basic premise of the *Lehrstück* is that it was designed to be performed without an audience: the actors are also the spectators. As Peter W. Ferran notes:

> Without an audience's perceptual experience and response – its *reception* – there is theoretically no true play, no 'dramatic event'. Nor is this practicing activity a rehearsal, for rehearsal also implies preparing a performance for an eventual audience.[125]

Instead, this is an exercise, a way of working through one's relationship to the events that unfold in the play. Such flexibility led one group of students to ask 'what if [the Agitators] are lying? [. . .] What if what they are describing *never happened*?'[126] The possibilities are open when the playtext is not restricted by the guiding hand, or indeed the ham-fist, of a single director. This new approach to performance leads Benton Jay Komins to conclude that 'through its experimental confinement, plasticity of roles, and multiple layers of representation, the play exceeds the message of any regime, ethics, or ideology'.[127] So, if the performance of the playtext doesn't require someone to instruct the actors, how is it to be read under this section's heading?

The central episodes of the play chart the Young Comrade's continued inability to carry out the *Agitators'* instructions. Initially, the Young Comrade is happy and, more importantly, able to follow their instructions. In terms of the power relations in the play, the structure is clear. The Control Chorus is the Party. It delegates its power to the Agitators, who are only equipped with the teachings of the Marxist classics and the attitudes and skills required to bring about a revolution. The Young Comrade accepts this position, which is set out clearly in the first scene, and in the second, accepts the practical action required:

---

[124] See, for example, Theodor Adorno, 'Commitment', in Adorno et al, *Aesthetics and Politics* (London: Verso, 2007), pp. 177–95 (182) or Rainer Friedrich, 'Brecht and Postmodernism', *Philosophy and Literature* 23: 1 (1999), pp. 44–64 (59).

[125] Peter W. Ferran, 'New Measures for Brecht in America', *Theater*, 25: 2 (1994), pp. 9–23 (20).

[126] As reported by their tutor, Ian Maxwell, in 'Teaching Performance Studies with Brecht's *Lehrstück* Model: *The Measures Taken*', *Brecht Yearbook*, 41 (2019), pp. 76–97 (79).

[127] Benton Jay Komins, 'Rewriting, Violence, and Theater: Bertolt Brecht's *The Measures Taken* and Heiner Müller 's *Mauser*', *The Comparatist*, 26 (2002), pp. 99–119 (105).

to obliterate his own identity in the name of the cause. The problems start in the third, and I will focus on this because it sets out how the Young Comrade is unable to follow the Agitators' instructions most clearly.

The Agitators' first task for the Young Comrade is quite straightforward. They observe some 'coolies', the disparaging and dated word used in the playtext for unskilled workers, dragging a barge with rice, who fall over because the ground is slippery. They tell the Young Comrade to inform the workers of boots available that will stop them from slipping and getting beaten by their overseer. They expressly state: 'But don't let yourself become sorry for them!'. One Agitator plays the Overseer, two more the Coolies, and the other the Young Comrade. Before anything happens, the Coolies sing a song that pulls at the Young Comrade's heart strings; he notes: 'How hideous to hear the lovely way these men cloak the torment of their work.'[128] One of the Coolies slips over and the Young Comrade acknowledges his own problem: 'It is hard to look at these men without feeling sorry for them' (70). This is a moment of *anagnorisis*, the classical Greek term of recognition that Aristotle identified as a key process in the realization of a tragedy. I will return to this idea presently. Yet the Young Comrade does overcome his emotions and delivers the text provided by the Agitators, that is, speaking the words of other people. The Coolies agree with him, but the Overseer says that the rice will not reach its destination on time and so whips them to continue their drudgery. Under the weight of this suffering, the Young Comrade's resolve crumbles and he keeps placing a large stone on the Coolies' path so that they do not slip any more. The Overseer draws the conclusion that he would 'sooner have your tender-hearted comrade' (71) than fetch boots from farther afield. As the journey continues, the Young Comrade exhausts himself with the exertion and asks the Coolies to demand the boots. This arouses the Overseer's scepticism and he accuses the Young Comrade of being an agitator. Consequently, the Agitators could not show their faces in that part of the city and their work was seriously set back.

The episode charts a process worthy of our attention. The Young Comrade is given clear instructions, which are themselves not revolutionary, but reformist. Reform perpetuates an existing system, whereas revolution destroys it in favour of a new one. The latter is often the aim of Marxist revolutionaries, but their first stratagem is a savvy one: they realize that they cannot simply make a revolution, but need to cultivate an attitude of reform to show that change is possible. The Young Comrade is not being asked to do something terribly daring. However, as Oliver Simons observes, 'it becomes clear that political agitation in Brecht's

---

[128] Bertolt Brecht, *The Decision*, John Willett (trans.), in Brecht, John Willett (ed.), *Collected Plays*, volume 3, (London: Bloomsbury, 1997), pp. 61–89 (both quotations 69). Subsequent references to the playtext will appear as bracketed page numbers in the main text.

learning play cannot be differentiated from aesthetic concepts, as "error" [*hamartia*] and "pity" [*elios*] are two seminal categories of drama according to Aristotle'.[129] Even in 1955, the year before he died, Brecht emphasized that his theatre was 'non-Aristotelian'.[130] Simons, countering Brecht's position, makes a powerful argument that situates the *Lehrstück* at an aporia between an old and a new theatre: 'The paradox of the young comrade [...] is that he desires to act in a play whose rules [i.e. those of the *Lehrstück*] he clearly does not yet know because they are different than those possible in theater. In this impossibility of his action he is pulverized'.[131] The connection between dramatic form and dramatic content helps to illuminate the problems that lead to the Young Comrade's political killing.

It is clearly not the case that the Young Comrade does not want to carry out the Agitators' instructions; he states that he agrees with them before the episode is reenacted. The conflict arises when theory, his intention, is brought into contact with practice, the reality of the situation. The Agitators exhort him to dismiss his perfectly human feelings in the name of the greater good, but it turns out that that is easier said than done. The persistence of the ancient tragic devices in Brecht's new dramatic form mirrors the stubbornness of the Young Comrade's feelings for those who are suffering. And it was this that led to his politicization in the first place: 'My heart beats for the Revolution. The sight of injustice made me join the ranks of the militants' (63).

The Agitators, however, do not have this problem. In the eighth and final scene, they execute the Young Comrade and burn his body in a lime pit because their revolutionary work will come to nothing if he is discovered and identified. They proceed rationally and wish to include the Young Comrade in that they seek his agreement, although the Second Agitator also notes: 'But even if he does not agree he must vanish and vanish entirely' (88). The Young Comrade does agree, but only after one of the few explicit pauses in the playtext's stage directions. The pause may suggest that he actually does agree or that he has no choice, but to agree. Either way, the Agitators demonstrate their distance from both older models of tragedy and older modes of behaviour: they follow their own instructions to the letter.

The Decision invites readers and participants in the *Lehrstück* to consider what is required to carry out the Agitators' instructions (which repeat and vary

---

[129] Oliver Simons, 'Theater of Revolution and the Law of Genre. Bertolt Brecht's *The Measures Taken (Die Maßnahme)*, *The Germanic Review*, 84: 4 (2009), pp. 327–52 (335).

[130] Bertolt Brecht, 'Can the Present-Day World Be Reproduced by Means of Theatre?', in Marc Silberman, Steve Giles and Tom Kuhn (eds.), *Brecht on Theatre*, third edition, (London: Bloomsbury, 2014) pp. 311–2 (312).

[131] Simons, 'Theater of Revolution', p. 340.

themselves in scenes four to six). Brecht emphasizes in scene four that the Young Comrade has learned from his mistake with the Coolies, and in scene five, his analysis of how a rich Merchant's trade works is accurate, so he is no fool; it is not a lack of understanding that leads to his demise. The play thus offers much to consider in terms of what happens to instructions given in everyday life. Here the instructions are overt,[132] but the Young Comrade is unable to carry them out, unlike P in *Catastrophe*, who consciously defies his instructions. In the latter play, the focus is far more on the consequences of not conforming to instructions. In *The Decision*, the consequences are clear, but we are invited to ask why the Young Comrade cannot overcome the humanism that led him to join the Party. Both plays engage metatheatrical structures (the persistence of Aristotelian tragedy and the doubling of audiences and directors, respectively) to contextualize and further problematize the process of following instructions. As such, the issues raised are not treated in simplistic terms, but are presented as a complex challenge for their readerships and audiences.

4 Actors Perform to Live Audiences

Validation Required

It is broadly acknowledged that for theatre to take place, a live audience is required.[133] Even in the example of the *Lehrstück*, which abolished the strict distinction between actor and spectator, those not acting become live spectators to the action. This element of the theatrical event distinguishes theatre from television and film. It means that any performance is subject to a direct response. It also creates a dynamic relationship that is the complement to the previous section's process, as exemplified at the conclusion of *Catastrophe*. Here, a director's instructions are followed to the letter and produce the desired effect: rapturous applause from the audience. When the protagonist intervenes, the situation changes radically and the approval quickly dissipates. It is unclear, however, whether this signals approval's opposite, opprobrium, or a shock that leads to a more careful reflection on the dramatic scene.

The relationship between instruction, its processing by the actor, and its reception by a live audience is impossible to legislate for, as any actor or director will testify. Rehearsal conceptualizes and refines a series of choices, which are then embodied, often in the hope that they will have their desired effect. But how many times have lines or actions considered funny in rehearsal

---

[132] However, as in everyday life, there are a number of covert rules in play here, too: the Young Comrade has to behave like a revolutionary, a role whose terms are specific, but implicit.

[133] See, for a recent example, Tobin Nellhaus, 'Online Role-Playing Games and the Definition of Theatre', *New Theatre Quarterly*, 33: 4 (2017), pp 345–59 (351–7).

elicited silence in performance? Or, conversely, when have sequences provoked laughter, when laughter was never intended? Consequently, although directors prepare productions and audiences provide responses, the latter can never be predicted and will actually depend on a range of factors that are beyond the theatre-makers' control. These factors can even vary from performance to performance, where a company can easily ask why something so successful on one night fell flat on another.

Helen Freshwater convincingly argues that we should neither underestimate the audience in its complexity nor consider it as a constituency that exclusively thinks about the performance. Instead, she notes that 'today many practitioners and scholars consider the bodily engagement of audiences to be something to explore, exploit and celebrate'.[134] This understanding articulates two important facets. First, it dispels the outdated view that spectators are in some way passive recipients of a performance. On the contrary, they are being presented with a wide range of stimuli that are impossible to ignore and that beg a response in some form. Second, the body itself is involved in the process. Laughter or revulsion, tension or catharsis are all physical reactions, and these will play their part in determining the way that spectators respond to the experience of a performance.

One of an audience's functions is, at one end of the spectrum, to validate the work they see and, at the other, to reject it. Yet theatre audiences are also collectives, and spectators can feel the weight of peer pressure to approve of a show that they did not necessarily enjoy as much as more vociferous others. Validation is thus more difficult to gauge than it may at first appear.

More generally, as Caroline Heim puts it, audiences 'take on a specific role in giving feedback to the actors onstage. This is not a conscious choice but it occurs because theatre is a live encounter between two troupes'.[135] There is, of course, a vast range of responses available to the spectator, with indifference marking a form of rejection that may lack the visceral fervour of audible booing. And the unconscious element suggests that responses may tap into ideological positions the spectator may not knowingly register.

Approval or disapproval can also manifest itself elsewhere. Spectators can vote with their feet, both in the specific context of a performance by leaving either sometime in a show or during one of its intervals. Similarly, they can receive prior responses, in reviews or by word of mouth, that either encourage them to buy a ticket or resolve them to avoid a particular production. These examples already gesture to a problem regarding audiences: it is difficult to divine whether a response is that of an individual or one inflected by group

---

[134] Helen Freshwater, *Theatre & Audience* (London: Methuen, 2009), p. 19.

[135] Caroline Heim, *Audience as Performer: The Changing Role of Theatre Audiences in the Twenty-First Century* (London: Routledge, 2016), p. 24.

memberships and collective sensibilities. And so, while Kirsty Sedgman sensitively interrogates the problems of audience research,[136] I am more concerned with the dynamics of the process: what an audience is being asked and how it might respond.

The process of actors playing to live audiences also maps onto any exchange that takes place in everyday life, where the live performance of a role will elicit a response. Butler's ideas of gender performativity, as noted in the previous section, can provide a useful example. That is, she notes that gender is both constituted *and* policed. The policing is conducted by the audience to the performance. I provided some examples in the previous section, but the practice of social policing, as one might call it, extends into all aspects of one's life. Using an inappropriate word or term may provoke a scowl or a raised eyebrow, if not a direct challenge. Conversely, an approved sentiment may simply be marked by the unimpeded flow of a conversation, or by more overt expressions, such as a nod, a smile, or an embrace.

On the stage, this theatrical process has a different dynamic in that, for the most part, actors perform and the audience responds. In communicative exchange in the everyday world, performers and audiences alternate, depending on who is speaking. The process itself is one of continual interchange. That is, one may unintentionally say something that offends the listener, who responds with a show of disapproval, yet this show will elicit its own response from the original speaker, perhaps acknowledging the social *faux pas* or defending it. (And the perceived *faux pas* will itself contravene the social rules or instructions considered in the previous section.) The everyday application of this final process, then, cannot be divorced from the overt and covert instructions that we receive as social subjects. And this process can also be found onstage, in the dialogues the audience experience. There is thus always someone performing and someone representing an onstage audience in every dialogue.

Playtexts clearly have ways to acknowledge that they are playing to a live audience. Direct address is the most obvious form, although the aside, which temporarily grants access for a figure to address the audience while others remain in the stage world, is also available. However, it is rarer for playtexts to point to the dynamic alternation between performer and audience in dialogue. This may occur when performance draws attention to itself, as in courtroom dramas where the quality of a testimony or a legal argument is analysed by an onstage audience, but I will return to this idea in the Conclusion. The two examples I have chosen, below, represent two quite distinct uses of direct

---

[136] See Katie Sedgman, 'Audience Experience in an Anti-expert Age: A Survey of Theatre Audience Research', *Theatre Research International*, 42: 3 (2018), pp. 307–22.

address, a clear signal that the actors are playing to a live audience. The first presents the device's more conventional function, explicitly inviting the audience to make judgements; the second, as we shall see, does something quite different.

Aeschylus, *Eumenides*

While I have selected contemporary plays, or at least those of the twentieth century, as my examples in previous sections, I return to the dawn of Western theatre-making by focussing on *Eumenides* (premiere 458 BCE). This is a play that considers legal upheaval. Previously, the murder of a parent was punished by the Furies, supernatural creatures that hunted down the perpetrator and administered terrible punishment. This system, of course, had some clear limitations: the perpetrator was unable to offer a defence or any evidence, and the process was thus one of mechanical vengeance. In *Eumenides*, we follow Orestes, who has killed his mother, Clytemnestra, and is pursued by the Furies for his crime. However, the murder itself is complicated. Orestes is protected by the god Apollo, who also supported the murder. In order to resolve the tension, the goddess Athena constitutes a court of law at which a decision can be reached, with a jury made up of Athenian citizens. The jury is unable to reach a clear verdict and Athena, having already given her reason for supporting Orestes, acquits him. The Furies are furious, yet Athena manages to convince them to adopt a new role in Athenian society, one honoured, not feared, by the citizenry. A Chorus of Women sing their praises and escort them out of the theatre in a ceremonial procession.

The play introduces the audience to a new set of judicial practices and the audience is addressed directly on several occasions. The opening speech, delivered by the Pythia, the priestess of Apollo, begins with ritual praise for the gods before she asks, 'Where are the Greeks among you?'[137] She then proceeds to describe the terror and horror of the Furies. The drama then unfolds without direct address to the audience, while a great deal of exposition sets out, implicitly, an amount of backstory for the audience. The Furies are the first chorus the audience encounter, and they have a long set of speeches, addressing the audience as was the convention, setting out their juridical rights and thereby attempting to convince the audience of their rightfulness to perpetuate them. A subsequent choral chant explicitly uses 'you' and 'your' (254 and 255, respectively) to make a direct appeal. Athena then implicates the audience in

---

[137] Aeschylus, *The Eumenides*, in Aeschylus, *The Oresteia. Agamemnon, The Libation Bearers, The Eumenides*, tr. by Robert Fagles (London: Penguin, 1977), pp. 225–77 (232). Subsequent references to the playtext will appear as bracketed page numbers in the main text.

the legal process using an inclusive 'our' (255) and advises 'my city' that 'silence is best' (256) during the trial. Apollo also implicates the audience when he says, 'You have heard what you have heard' (261) in a line that equally addresses the jury members and the audience. Orestes also joins in when he exits as a free man, bidding 'farewell, [Athena] and the people of your city' (266). And in the final section of the play, Athena includes 'my people' (267) and 'the mortals of my city' (270) in her plan for the Furies' new role. The frequent involvement of the audience in the transition from one form of justice to another makes them more than mere spectators to the action; they are actively encouraged to process the different positions, but this is not an exclusively cerebral activity. The Pythia's role already promotes a visceral response; she is effectively the Furies' warm-up, disturbing the spectators before the dark figures finally enter the scene. A combination of rational reflection and emotive reactions follows as the playtext oscillates between accounts of the murder and its psychological repercussions.

The route that Aeschylus offers, however, is not a simple one. Edith Hall notes how different the trial is from our usual expectations in that

> no agreement is reached before the trial about the number of votes necessary for a determination to be reached. The crime of which Orestes is accused is not described or analyzed; no witnesses to it are called. The assault on Clytemnestra's character is of questionable relevance, and her motivation for killing Agamemnon (the sacrifice of Iphigenia) is excluded from discussion.[138]

Such inconsistencies lead to a number of challenges for the audience. In addition, Apollo makes a fanciful assertion, contending that mothers are not in fact parents, but mere incubators of a father's seed. Athena's grounds for casting her vote in favour of Orestes is similarly odd: she says that she honours 'the male' (264) because she was not born of woman. Eric Dugdale and Loramy Gerstbauerpolis thus argue that the verdict does not resolve the plot, but adds complication.[139] Hall also notes how the new system retains features of the old, rather than abolishing them, thus acknowledging the complexity of the new arrangement.[140] Peter J. Steinberger places this in the context of recent research into Homeric and Athenian societies, stating that they were far more complex than previously thought, providing a diverse audience for the theatre, too. He concludes:

---

[138] Edith Hall, 'Peaceful Conflict Resolution and Its Discontents in Aeschylus's *Eumenides*', *Common Knowledge*, 21: 2 (2015), pp. 253–69 (268).

[139] Eric Dugdale and Loramy Gerstbauerpolis, 'Forms of Justice in Aeschylus' *Eumenides*', *Polis*, 34 (2017), pp. 226–50 (229).

[140] See Hall, 'Peaceful Conflict Resolution', p. 262.

The intellectual system of the *Eumenides*, as a product of its time, could not but encompass both the explicit structure of metaphysical coherence that kept society more or less whole and the sort of frequently implicit elements of discord and disagreement that will be characteristic of any discursive universe and that give rise to precisely the kinds of hard cases that form the typical subject matter of tragedy.[141]

Eumenides is not the presentation of one system's superiority over the other. Rather, it is a problematization of that new system, a reckoning that, on the one hand, suggests its advantages over automatic vengeance, but also points to the contentious roles of the adversaries and the compromised nature of the ultimate arbiter of the case.

But this is not a thought experiment, a disinterested reflection on how justice might work. The court corresponds to the real Areopagus that tried cases of murder, among other things. The link is made explicit in the final procession out of the theatre into the city. As Pat Easterling shows, 'the value of such associations is that they link the stage action with the watching community's present and future, by suggesting a continuity of ritual for the well-being of the city and a hoped-for continuity in order and prosperity'.[142] The space between theatre and the outside world collapses in the final moments of the play.

Eumenides engages the audience with a number of contradictory ideas and feelings regarding the pursuit of justice. The playtext provides no helpful nudges, but instead heaps difficulty on difficulty, provoking an active deliberation and acknowledging that solely rational decisions ignore other factors integral to the way that we process experiences and act on them.

Jackie Sibblies Drury, *Fairview*

Fairview (premiere 2018) is a complex play that only addresses its audience directly in its final pages, although there are a couple of comic asides earlier in the playtext. In order to approach the acknowledgement that the actors are playing to a live audience, I will consider the play's three-act form and the way that it employs the three other processes that I maintain constitute theatricality.

The first act '*appears* to be a comedic family drama' (my emphasis).[143] Here, the Frasiers, a comfortable middle-class Black family, consisting of mother and

---

[141] Peter J. Steinberger, 'Eumenides and the Invention of Politics', *Polis*, 39 (2022), pp. 77–98 (84).

[142] Pat Easterling, 'Theatrical Furies. Thoughts on *Eumenides*', in Martin Revermann and Peter Wilson (eds.), *Performance, Iconography, Reception: Studies in Honour of Oliver Taplin* (Oxford: Oxford University Press, 2008), pp. 219–36 (233).

[143] Jackie Sibblies Drury, *Fairview* (New York: Theatre Communications Group, 2019), p. 5. Subsequent references to the playtext will appear as bracketed page numbers in the main text.

father Beverly and Dayton, daughter Keisha and Beverly's sister Jasmine, prepare a meal for Beverly's mother's birthday. Damon Krometis notes that they 'lead relatively mundane lives full of low-stakes challenges',[144] but this only gives a partial view of the rigorously constructed first act. A more careful account reveals several features of comic dramaturgy that are recognizable from television sitcoms.

The genre is established early when Dayton fails to provide the right cutlery for the meal, and then Beverly says, 'Everything must be perfect today' (9), inviting the comic doom that will inevitably follow. Here, she speaks the words of other people in such a familiar cue. Later, Jasmine, the comically contrary sister, performs a satirical contradiction by saying that she is faddishly avoiding dairy products and then takes a bite of cheese. Beverly's son, Tyrone, contributes to the conscious stock design of the first act by phoning through that he will not be able to make the meal because his flight has been rerouted, another comic obstacle to Beverly's 'perfect day'. There is even a two-page routine that shows how conscious the stock characters are themselves of their ability to play out standard structures. Here, Beverly asks Dayton whether he bought the root vegetables, to which he replies, 'Um –' (19) as an implied apology. What follows is Beverly's comically detailed and protracted recounting of the dialogue she had had with Dayton to ensure that he bought the right produce. At its conclusion, Dayton presents the vegetables with a flourish: 'Ta-da!' (20). He consciously plays the role of the impractical husband in order to disappoint it. At the act's conclusion, the farcical action reaches its climax when Keisha announces that the cake has burnt. Beverly faints, Dayton and Jasmine look on in horror, and Keisha dashes in. The careful maintenance of the genre itself also suggests that the characters are following their instructions correctly.

As Kyle C. Frisina notes, the first act 'draws careful attention to the act of looking at blackness',[145] but this is a very specific kind of blackness. It is one that is in no way natural. It is not fly-on-the-wall realism, but a consciously constructed set of dialogues and actions that play up to a certain kind of entertainment. The actors are there to please us with their antics. That this is directed to an at least part-white audience[146] becomes evident in the second act.

Here, the audience sees the action of the first act repeating itself, but hears four white voices: Suze, Jimbo, Mack and Bets, having a very different

---

[144] Damon Krometis, 'Sitting on the Couch: The Conundrum of Spectatorship in Jackie Sibblies Drury's *Fairview*', *Journal of Dramatic Theory and Criticism*, 37: 1 (2022), pp. 67–86 (73).

[145] Kyle C. Frisina, 'Contemporary African-American Drama at Visuality's Limits', *Modern Drama* 63: 2 (2020), pp. 197–220 (202).

[146] Michael Pearce, quoting Drury, notes that for the play to work at all, at least some white audience members are a prerequisite, in 'Making Whiteness Visible and Felt in *Fairview*', *Humanities*, 10: 2 (2021), pp. 1–16 (2).

conversation. In it, they discuss the question of which race they would choose to be if they were not white. The question is, of course, ludicrous and this is signalled at certain points in the exchange. Mack, for example, sees race as a kind of clothing, rather than a lived experience, and asks what effects it would have on 'who I actually am' (41). None of the voices can conceive that their question divides body and mind, and so this becomes a running joke throughout the act. That the question itself is fundamentally racist is never entertained, and this blithe ignorance is also comical. That is because the voices are expressions of what has been called 'new racism'. This is a form of racism that is not as overt as using slurs to signal a racist position. Rather, as Robin DiAngelo defines, it is 'the ways in which racism has adapted over time so that modern norms, policies, and practices result in similar racial outcomes as those in the past, while not appearing to be explicitly racist'.[147] So, Jimbo seeks Mack's 'consent' (39) before asking the question, asking permission when Mack is not actually aware of what he is consenting to. Mack then offers to inject specious precision into the discussion in a bid to legitimize it. He asks whether they are talking about 'race' or 'ethnicity' (40) and proposes that he would assume a politically correct 'Latinx' identity rather than a 'Latino' one (41). Although the dialogue is apparently spontaneous, it nonetheless sounds so clichéd that it is clear that they are all speaking the words of other people, an indictment of their second-hand discourse.

There are also clear parallels between the dialogue and the forms and structure of the first act. Suze, for example, initially says that she will not answer the racist question, but then later does so when opting for African American as her race of choice. This echoes Jasmine's frequent comic hypocrisy when she says one thing and does another. It is also no coincidence that Mack's and Bets' voices 'enter' at the same time as a new figure enters the stage for the first time (Jasmine for Mack, and Keisha for Bets). Synchronization with the stage action also highlights the unwittingly comical nature of the dialogue. So, when Suze delivers her extended defence of choosing an African-American identity, the end of the speech explicitly coincides with Dayton's 'Ta-da!'.

The second act not only plays over the first, it actually mirrors it in a variety of ways that expose the absurd positions the white voices claim as reasonable. The act follows the same theatricality of the first act (actors play roles, as each of the voices adopts a sadly familiar approach to racial questions; they very much speak the words of others; and they obey a series of rules – here, a debased form of political correctness – in order to carry the dialogue). Yet in this act, the

---

[147] Robin DiAngelo, 'New Racism', *Counterpoints*, 398 (2012), pp. 105–32 (106).

comedy is enhanced by the apparent seriousness of the discussion. That is, as long as you are not a white member of the audience.

Michael Pearce reports his own reactions as a white spectator to the second act: 'I found listening to the white characters' obliviousness to their own racism and privilege excruciating. Yet, I found myself silently participating in it at the same time. It prompted me to think about how I might respond to their questions and comments.' He elaborates that his insinuation in the piece 'was not achieved through empathy, but through affinity – we never felt for the white characters, but we were prompted to feel like them'.[148] This is a quite remarkable achievement. The use of voices, contrasted with the performance of staged Black bodies, provoked a proximity and a distance in white spectators who disagreed with the voices' sentiments.

The third act dialectically synthesizes the first and the second. Here, the Frasiers' comedy continues, but the white voices gradually appear on stage in person with Bets attempting to play a sympathetic version of Beverly's mother. Jimbo later enters as Tyrone. In the first act, we learned that Tyrone was a successful lawyer; Jimbo transforms him into a foul-mouthed beer-drinker. Mack then arrives as Keisha's schoolfriend Erika, 'dressed like a drag version of a black teenage girl' (86) and Bets doubles as a sexy, jazz singer rendition of Beverly's mother. Over the course of this act, the white characters infect the action with their own racist interpretations of Black life, lowering the Frasiers' class and behaviours to conform to their second-hand views of Black people. Interestingly, the Frasiers know that there is something wrong, but cannot identify the problem. Keisha had already registered a discomfort in the first act when she says: 'But I feel like something is keeping me from all that. / Something . . . / [. . .] And that something. / It thinks that it has made me who I am' (27). This consciousness that all is not well returns in act three. Keisha notes her discomfort in an aside, but the convention is violated when Bets expresses her sympathy, shocking Keisha. The action continues and culminates in a destructive food fight, the product of the adolescent interlopers. What follows is a moment of crisis.

Keisha initiates an aside with Suze, who is still playing her grandmother. Keisha calls a halt to the dialogue, and everyone now listens to her. Keisha says to Suze, 'I can't hear anything but you staring at me' (100). The white gaze is preventing Keisha from articulating herself and thinking clearly. Keisha then addresses the audience directly, and this takes up the final five pages of the playtext. She invites the audience members who identify as white to come onto the stage so that the Black actors can go down into the auditorium and join the

---

non-white spectators. Soon after, she refers to the white-identifying spectators as 'them', and so she is clearly addressing the non-white audience, even if white-identifying spectators have not accepted the invitation. She also points to the transitory nature of the situation when she says, 'Could I tell them that those seats are not theirs, / even though they paid for them? / That no one can own a seat forever? / That no one should' (103). She concludes by trying to tell a story about Black people and keeps failing, and ends up describing a life of endeavour and struggle. At its conclusion, these people try to see things from different perspectives trying to achieve the play's title, a self-referential fair view.

The invitation to white-identifying spectators to take to the stage is clearly a different form of engagement from that of *Eumenides*. Yet there are two features of the invitation that retain an interesting ambivalence. First, Keisha asks the non-white audience, 'Would it help if I told them that the show is ending?' (102), and then she encourages the white-identifying spectators to participate because their white stage manager, Terri, is also coming up (103). I suggest that the ambivalence comes from two possible interpretations. On the one hand, Keisha seems desperate to have the white-identifying spectators participate and entices them with incentives (it won't take long and other people are doing it). On the other, the encouragement draws attention to the fact that Keisha has to offer incentives, that the white-identifying audience will not simply give up their privileges and subject themselves to being looked at. That the first exhortation is not directed to the target audience gestures to the latter interpretation, while the second one returns to a direct 'you', perhaps indicting the white constituency even further in that the first attempt did not achieve its ends.

Drury's intention seems clear, as Paul J. Edwards comments: 'The effect of white audience members coming to the stage is meant to make them a spectacle, undermining the white gaze created throughout the earlier moments of the play.' But he also notes some problems: as a person of colour, he had to make way for the white spectators who chose to partici-pate, reaffirming his passivity and lack of response. He also questions whether the remaining audience of colour can actually neither 'tell nor feel that they are no longer a spectacle'.[149] In addition, Pearce observes, as a white spectator of the production himself, that there is a weakness in appealing to white guilt in a liberal audience because 'it is a self-serving feeling which directs energy inwards, towards the person experiencing the

---

[149] Paul J. Edwards, 'Catering to White Audiences. *Fairview* at Woolly Mammoth', *The Drama Review*, 65: 2 (2021), pp. 173–8 (both 176).

emotion and away from the problem that triggered it in the first place'.[150] That is, the spectators are too busy negotiating their own feelings to look at the broader structures that construct such feelings. Krometis counters that Keisha's challenge may bring about a different effect 'by asking white spectators to stand onstage and have their whiteness viewed as strange. This moment of invitation is transgressive, exposing how spectatorship is coded by white people as a racially privileged act'.[151] He also calls the act a 'role reversal' in which 'white spectators might feel they have proven they could not possibly be racist, and therefore distance themselves from any negative feelings the play elicits'.[152] While participation could indeed be considered tokenistic,[153] I would like to linger on the idea of role reversal.

Power relationships are, by definition, asymmetrical, with one side having more power than the other. But this is not a one-way street. As Hegel's meditations on the master and servant relationship revealed, the relationship is a negotiated one in which the master's power is recognized by the servant. This is why such relationships do not persist – they are unstable and ripe for modification. However, inverting a power relationship does not reverse the roles; they are only renegotiated. And so the white-identifying audience will not share the feelings of being watched experienced by the Black actors on stage or the Black spectators in their everyday lives. But they will have participated in a collective action that places them into an unfamiliar context and will have to deal with the consequences.

Fairview is a remarkable play in its acknowledgement that the actors are playing to a live audience. Unlike *Eumenides*, it does not seek the audience's judgement. Instead, it seeks to destroy the illusion of the monolithic audience, not only making it aware of racial differences, but also conducting a sociological experiment in every performance to gauge the proportion of white-identifying spectators who mount the stage and those who remain seated. This division will also, however, have taken place earlier, due to the indirect acknowledgement of the audience. The different racial constituencies will respond differently to the stylized domestic comedy, but even more so to the racist dialogue of the second act. The play presages the direct address at its conclusion, by implicitly dividing the audience well in advance and inducing it to reflect on its racially inflected responses.

---

[150] Pearce, 'Making Whiteness Visible', p. 5.   [151] Krometis, 'Sitting on the Couch', p. 68.
[152] Ibid., p. 77.   [153] See Pearce, 'Making Whiteness Visible', p. 14.

Conclusion

Theatricality as Interdependent Processes

The four sections of this Element have each focussed on a single theatrical process. Yet readers will have noticed that separating them out inevitably downplays the ways that they inform each other. When an actor plays a role, that role will be structured by a discourse, a language which, by definition, did not originate in that speaker. The role will also be subject to a variety of laws, rules and conventions – the instructions provided by a third party. And that role will be subject to live responses, in the form of language and/or gestures. Revisiting any of the sections will reveal the interdependence of the four processes. Indeed, discussing direct address in *Fairview* was impossible without contextualizing it with respect to the other processes. Consequently, the method I have proposed for investigating theatricality in playtexts needs to be executed in the round, with due sensitivity to the more prominent processes while appreciating that the others will also be involved because, ultimately, they inform and regulate each other to a greater or lesser extent.

The idea of regulation moves theatricality, as understood in this Element, as a set of material processes, into a more explicitly political sphere. Here, I understand politics as 'the important, inescapable, and difficult attempt to determine relations of power in a given space', to cite Stefan Collini's definition.[154] The task is 'inescapable' because politics pervades all relationships, and it is 'difficult' because these relationships are both hard to articulate and subject to change over time. The 'attempt' becomes a playwright's contingent approach to structuring the playtext in such a way that the chosen forms of representation are appropriate to the reality being represented. And because the political is predicated on the 'relations of power', it is sensible to examine how power might flow through the prisms of the four processes.

Each process signifies a constraint on a key ideological position that has accompanied the growth of capitalism over the past centuries: individualism.[155] Realo et al. propose three components involved in constructing this discourse: autonomy, mature self-responsibility and uniqueness.[156] Each of these categories is compromised by the four theatrical processes. In terms of roles, language available, instructions provided (overtly or covertly) and their policing by

---

[154] Stefan Collini, 'Defending Cultural Criticism', *New Left Review*, 18 (2002), https://newleftreview .org/issues/ii18/articles/stefan-collini-defending-cultural-criticism [accessed 29 August 2023].

[155] For a more extensive discussion, see David W. Bromley, *Possessive Individualism. A Crisis of Capitalism* (Oxford: Oxford University Press, 2019).

[156] Anu Realo, Kati Koido, Eva Ceulemans, Jüri Allik, 'Three Components of Individualism', *European Journal of Personality*, 16: 3 (2002), pp. 163–84 (167–8).

others, the individual's autonomy is comprehensively limited. All the categories, of course, evolve over time but still represent significant curtailments to autonomy. Mature self-responsibility is also dependent on a set of contexts that the individual does not create. And while each individual is indisputably unique – no one shares either the same DNA or experience of the world – such uniqueness is only of limited categorical value. For example, uniqueness has been radically called into question when confronted by the big data revolution of the previous years. For all one's uniqueness, one's behaviour has become ever more foreseeable through the development of predictive analytics, where the collection of massed data from individuals accurately models behaviours.[157]

That the processes associated with making theatre reproduce themselves in everyday life creates a powerful connection between the analysis of playtexts and their implications for the ways we understand, approach and interact with society. Yet, so far, my analyses have only taken playtexts in which the four processes have been prominent and clear to identify. My contention, however, was that these processes precede the theatre itself and thus, they should be identifiable even when they do not draw attention to themselves.

Are All Playtexts Theatrical?

As far back as Abel's first investigation into metatheatre, he noted, 'If we understand metatheatre as the moment when the theatre comes to itself, it is no longer surprising that it is almost impossible for the theatre not to become metatheatre.'[158] Eggington makes the argument more explicitly:

> there can be no theater that is not already a metatheater, in that in the instant a distinction is recognized between a real space and another imaginary one that mirrors it, that very distinction becomes an element to be incorporated as another distinction in the imaginary space's work of mimesis. [. . .] Therefore, while there are plenty of plays that do not refer explicitly to the theater, all plays that share in this representational structure are characterized by this potential.[159]

The theatre is a hall of mirrors, supported by a structure that always threatens to implicate the real space from which it is being watched. So, what happens when we investigate a playtext that does not exhibit its theatrical processes overtly?

---

[157] See, for example, Vaibhav Kumar and M. L. Garg, 'Predictive Analytics: A Review of Trends and Techniques', *International Journal of Computer Applications*, 182: 1 (2018), pp. 31–7.

[158] Abel, *Tragedy and Metatheatre*, p. 13. Hornby agrees, in *Drama, Metadrama, and Perception*, pp. 31–2.

[159] Eggington, *How the World Became a Stage*, p. 74.

Naturalism may offer a suitable field of enquiry. It originally understood itself as a kind of experiment, mixing together different substances, understood sociologically (such as sex, class, particular biographical experiences, etc.), to see what would happen. Human beings were put under the lens of scientific investigation, just as one would study animals in nature. However, 'science' is not a neutral term, and there was a strong sense of determinism inflecting these ideas. As Émile Zola put it, 'I am waiting for environment to determine the characters and the characters to act according to the logic of facts combined with the logic of their own disposition.'[160] In order to engender the dispassionate gaze, the audience was not directly acknowledged, and because the act of observation was so crucial, the stage rarely explicitly offered an interrogation of reality, but rather its reproduction. As such, naturalism did not explicitly point to the four theatrical processes or highlight them in its playtexts.

The middle classes also feature prominently in naturalist drama, but, as Bernd Stegemann observes in a discussion of their role in theatre, 'the bourgeoisie was shaped as a class in that it was forced into individual isolation [*Vereinzelung*] due to its alienation from its own life', developing individualism as a justificatory ideology.[161] The concept of authenticity then arose as a way to paper over the contradiction between the characteristics of a class and the projections of its members as individuals: 'successfully producing the appearance of authenticity for the bourgeois class is like a seal of approval, that its idea of repression is working'.[162] Investigating the four theatrical processes in such plays may then allow us to look beyond the surface and reveal social mechanisms.

I have chosen to investigate Henrik Ibsen's *Ghosts*. At its heart are three bourgeois figures: Mrs Alving, the widow of Alderman Alving; her son Oswald, an artist who has returned to Norway from Paris; and Pastor Manders, a prominent protestant priest. The play deals with appearance and reality, in that Alderman Alving was a well-regarded pillar of the community, although he was sexually licentious. Indeed, Regina, the Alving's maid, is the result of his affair with another maid. It is also revealed that Oswald has inherited Alving's syphilis, not congenitally, but by puffing on his father's pipe as a child.[163] The subplot involves Engstrand, Regina's adoptive father, who has helped build an orphanage in Alving's name, initiated by Mrs Alving as a way of finally laying

---

[160] Émile Zola, 'Naturalism on the Stage', in Toby Cole (ed.), *Playwrights on Playwriting: From Ibsen to Ionesco* (New York: Cooper Square Press, 2001), pp. 5–14 (6).

[161] Bernd Stegemann, *Lob des Realismus* (Berlin: Theater der Zeit, 2015), p. 84.

[162] Ibid., p. 94.

[163] See Evert Sprinchorn, 'Syphilis in Ibsen's *Ghosts*', *Ibsen Studies*, 4: 2 (2004), pp. 191–204 (197–8).

the rumours about her husband to rest. However, the orphanage mysteriously burns down and Engstrand uses this to his advantage: Manders had persuaded Mrs Alving not to insure the building, and Engstrand effectively blackmails Manders into investing the money into his own project, a home for sailors, which is actually a thinly disguised brothel.

An analysis of the playtext reveals several instances of theatricality as understood as four interdependent processes. Before I consider the bourgeois figures, I offer the play's opening dialogue between Engstrand and Regina:

> REGINA (*keeping her voice low*): What do you want? Stay where you are! You're dripping wet!
> ENGSTRAND: It is God's blessed rain, my child.
> REGINA: The Devil's bloody rain, more like.
> ENGSTRAND: Why, Regina, the way you talk! (*Limps a few steps into the room.*) What I wanted to say is –
> REGINA: Here, you! Don't make such a noise with that foot. The young master's asleep upstairs.
> ENGSTRAND: In bed – at this hour? Why, the day's half gone.
> REGINA: That's none of your business.[164]

Regina's first and last lines challenge her father and reveal that she is comfortable in rejecting the role of the dutiful daughter. She also explicitly tells Engstrand how to behave, although the second stage direction shows her inability to enforce her instruction. That Engstrand does not object also says something important about the role of a working-class father at this point in Norway's social history. He also draws attention to the language Regina uses. Anne Marie Rekdal suggests that the tension between God and the Devil openly asks which supernatural entity rules the fictional world.[165] But if one analyses the two lines from the perspective that actors speak the words of other people, it is possible to detect that something else is at work here. Engstrand evokes divine nature, yet these words help construct an elaborate façade of godliness in a man who seeks to build a brothel and will blackmail a member of the clergy into financing it. Regina's riposte can then be understood as an automatic negation of her father's claim, not a heartfelt evaluation of the situation. Engstrand also attempts to play the onstage audience by criticizing Regina twice, but on both occasions, she defends her position and continues with her hostility towards

---

[164] Henrik Ibsen, *Ghosts*, student edition, Non Worrall (ed.), Michael Meyer (trans.) (Bloomsbury: London, 2008), p. 3. Subsequent references to the playtext will appear as bracketed page numbers in the main text.

[165] See Anne Marie Rekdal, 'The Freedom of Perversion. A Lacanian Reading of Ibsen's *Ghosts*', *Ibsen Studies*, 5: 2 (2005), pp. 121–47 (125).

him. In this opening dialogue, then, we can already identify the four theatrical processes and appreciate how they help the reader construct an account of unstable social relations.

Soon after, a brief exchange develops ideas about how role and power interact:

> MANDERS: Your father hasn't a very strong character,
> Miss Engstrand. He badly needs a hand to guide him.
> REGINA: Oh – yes, I dare say you're right there. (9)

Manders is socially superior to Regina and implicitly instructs her to look after her father. Regina, the onstage audience to her own decision, is initially caught out by the instruction – she registers her unwillingness in her 'oh'. However, she adopts the role of the dutiful daughter under duress, in contradistinction to the opening dialogue, deferring to Manders.

As one might expect from Stegemann's comments, social role itself is a key focus in this kind of theatre, as is the revelation of truth in line with naturalism's scientific thrust. Early on, Mrs Alving acknowledges to Manders that she has been playing a role regarding the reputation of her late husband and that the orphanage was an attempt to dispel the rumours swirling around him. It appears, then, that lies have been replaced by truth. However, if actors can *only* play roles, then revelations may not lead to truth in an absolute sense, but the adoption of new roles.

Act one ends with Mrs Alving looking on in horror as a relationship between the half-siblings Oswald and Regina develops. Act two opens with Mrs Alving and Manders noting how difficult it was to force down their meal, that is, they are still keeping up appearances in front of Oswald, and she acknowledges this clearly when she confides in Manders that 'If I were a real mother, I would take Oswald and say to him: "Listen, my boy. Your father was a degenerate –"' (30). She is both conscious of the role of mother and that she is playing it badly. It is for the audience, however, to ask why. She catches Manders himself role-playing the innocent shortly afterwards:

> MANDERS: I simply don't understand you.
> MRS ALVING: Oh, yes you do. (32)

And Manders admits as much when obliquely referencing his success in fending off his previous desires for Mrs Alving: 'It was my life's greatest victory, Helen. The victory over myself' (33), although he then goes on to contradict himself:

MRS ALVING: One forgets so easily what one was like.

MANDERS: I do not. I am the same as I always was. (ibid.)

He perpetuates the myth of the unchanging, sovereign individual, using language that verges on cliché, tapping into values that precede his utterances. Yet he also undermines this claim. On two occasions, he performs a neat pirouette. First, in act one he had argued that he would be pilloried as a clergyman for taking out insurance and not trusting in God. Yet when the orphanage is on fire, he declares, 'there blazes the judgement of God upon this sinful house!' (49). And in act three, Engstrand gives him a set of instructions regarding the funding of his sailors' home that shows Manders' remarkable mobility, not consistency, as he quickly moves from scepticism towards the home to full acceptance when pressurized.

Mrs Alving never stops switching roles. Towards the end of the play, she seemingly has a moment of *anagnorisis*, the recognition of a truth: 'They had taught me about duty and things like that, and I sat here for too long believing in them. In the end everything became a matter of duty' (55). Shortly after, however, Oswald upbraids her for both playing a role and speaking the words of others:

MRS ALVING: Yes, Oswald, I can, can't I? Oh, I could almost bless your sickness for bringing you home to me. I realise it now. You aren't mine. I must win you.

OSWALD: (*impatiently*) Yes, yes, yes. These are just empty phrases. (58)

By the end of the play, Mrs Alving is still a prisoner of her social role when she exclaims, 'I can't bear this!' (62) as her son drifts into oblivion – she has still not been able to tell him the truth about his father and his condition. *Anagnorisis* has not brought about a more honest relationship.

Ghosts has often been called a tragedy. Noting that the play echoes Sophocles' *Oedipus the King* in its approach to uncovering truths, K. M. Newton writes, '[Ibsen] is concerned like Sophocles with a universal human conflict, but one between human beings and social forms rather than between humanity and the god.'[166] Annamaria Cascetta agrees, invoking Ibsen's debt to Nietzsche and his views on tragedy.[167] Errol Durbach connects the process of discovery with Mrs Alving's merciless self-examination.[168] In

---

[166] K. M. Newton, *Modern Literature and the Tragic* (Edinburgh: Edinburgh University Press, 2008), p. 18.

[167] See Annamaria Cascetta, *Modern European Tragedy. Exploring Crucial Plays* (London: Anthem, 2014), p. 18.

[168] See Errol Durbach, 'The Dramatic Poetry of Ibsen's *Ghosts*', *Mosaic*, 11: 4 (1978), pp. 55–66 (56).

the light of a theatrical analysis of the play, however, I propose that, running very much counter to Ibsen's intentions, the play could productively be performed as a dark satirical comedy.

The importance of performance here is central because the playtext itself draws little attention to itself as 'theatrical'; only careful analysis has revealed its implicit theatricality. Consider the following exchange in which Manders challenges Mrs Alving about reading progressive literature, and whose speeches I have numbered for ease of reference:

1. MRS ALVING: But what do you object to in these books?
2. MANDERS: Object to? You surely don't imagine I spend my time studying such publications.
3. MRS ALVING: In other words, you've no idea what you're condemning?
4. MRS ALVING: I've read quite enough about these writings to disapprove of them.
5. MRS ALVING: Don't you think you ought to form your own opinion – ?
6. MRS ALVING: My dear Mrs Alving, there are many occasions in life when one must rely on the judgement of others. That is the way things are and it is good that it should be so. If it were not so, what would become of society?
7. MRS ALVING: Yes, yes. You may be right. (11–12)

In speeches one, three and five, Mrs Alving adopts the role of the enlightened, critical individual, asking rational questions and ridiculing the pastor for his ignorant rhetoric. There is already comedy in her exposure of the clergyman. Manders' response in speech six, the words after 'my dear Mrs Alving' could all be understood as quotations, drawing on commonplaces of the time. The surprise comes when Mrs Alving appears to agree with them in line seven. Surprise is at the heart of comic performance: a joke sets up its audience for one punchline and then delivers another.

In performance, naturalistic actors seek to reduce the gap between themselves and the characters they play to give the sense that they *are* the characters. The comic tradition of acting prefers to see characters as types, larger than the people we encounter in everyday life. Similarly, the Brechtian approach to understanding all speech as quotation (see Section 2) could lend the dialogues a heightened sense of artificiality. So, Mrs Alving's shift from speeches five to seven could be presented in a comically exaggerated manner. Having adopted the role of the middle-class rational liberal, she quickly transforms into the dutiful conservative.

By playing roles consciously and employing the performative means to make them clear, the audience is invited to observe the constructedness of the many positions the figures adopt. The positions themselves are built on a language that sustains them, and so as the role changes, so does the language. This represents another potentially comic switch if the language is delivered in speech marks. The roles are tested by the reception of the instructions, both implicit and explicit, that the figures give each other, again exposing the social rules at play. And the inconsistencies can elicit laughter in the audience. Such a reading turns the tragedy into a dark comedy. That is, the subject matter is grim: an innocent child will die because of the sins of his father. Yet these 'sins' are not an inevitable consequence of the father's actions. In the final act, Mrs Alving confesses to Oswald that it was not her husband's dissolution, but her puritanical devotion to duty that contributed to the play's problems: 'I made his home intolerable for your poor father' (55). And, as we learned in act one, it was Manders who instilled such dutifulness in Mrs Alving when she left her husband after a year of marriage. The play emphasizes social pressures over Alving's behaviour, indicting the social relations of the time.

The satire emerges from the perverse rules that the figures invoke and act on; they cause themselves endless misery and distress because they willingly follow the strictures, however changeable they may be. And when they have their moments of *anagnorisis*, the recognition leads to a different, yet equally unhelpful adoption of a new role that continues to perpetuate rather than to reconstruct the system within which they perform. It is not that we can get beyond playing roles, but we can seek out better ones that drain power from a figure like Manders and distribute it more fairly so that women like Mrs Alving are not forced endlessly to defer. The ghosts of the past materialize in the present, speaking lines long dead, but taken as living. The insights that emerge from a theatrical analysis of the play reveal it to be a comedy, littered with social absurdities that nonetheless lead to disaster. Laughing at them helps to reveal their contradictions and accounts for the workings of that society with a view to changing them.

Performance is thus the key to making the theatricality of apparently untheatrical playtexts visible. However, their textual analysis is the starting point. By seeking out covert instances of theatrical processes, one can understand how they might work and what kinds of approach to performance might be necessary both for revealing them and understanding their potential meanings.

The Politics of Theatricality

As already noted, theatricality is a political category. Its focus on the inescapability of role-playing, the words used to play those roles, the rules followed to play them correctly, and their reception in live exchanges exposes a complex network of power relations. The link of theatricality in the playtext and theatricality in everyday life offers a radical proposition for change.

Live theatre is dependent on the theatre's artifice. As an audience, we see theatrical performance through what Bert O. States calls 'a kind of binocular vision: one eye enables us to see the world phenomenally, the other eye enables us to see it significatively'.[169] That is, we know that actors are playing roles, but we can also draw meaning from what the roles play might represent. Or, as Dan Rebellato puts it: 'representational theatre is not illusionistic. In illusions we have *mistaken beliefs* about what we are seeing. No sane person watching a play believes that what is being represented before them is actually happening'.[170] As such, spectators are able to reconcile at least two realities at once and still leave a theatre having processed fictions as having meaningful resonances in the outside world.

As I argued in the Introduction, the troubling aspect of theatricality is that it extends beyond the theatre into our everyday lives. Here, 'mistaken beliefs' also play a significant role. Bruce Wilshire was unable to countenance the fact that we are always playing roles. It is a commonplace to assume that we speak language and that language does not speak us. It is disconcerting to believe that discrete individuals are far more similar to each other because they follow the same rules in the same ways, and that each time we speak we are performing to a live audience. Yet it *is* the case that the four theatrical processes pervade our social lives, and the implication of this is that society is just as artificial as the theatre. That is, it is a construction and nature plays the same role in it as it does in the theatre: real bodies are engaged in performance with all that that entails for those bodies. Work may tire them; felicitous circumstances may make them happy; injury may debilitate them, but death will finally make them inactive. The insight that naturalness is a veneer in terms of behaviour, belief and identity is both worrying and liberating. Clearly, to be told that something fixed is in fact fundamentally changeable will shake the stories we tell ourselves about ourselves. Yet, on the other hand, to be offered the possibility of transformation, that we do not have to put up with, say, the repressive and hypocritical authoritarianism of Pastor Manders, that more egalitarian distributions of power are available, would be a relief for many.

The theatre can represent not only its own theatricality to realize the effects discussed in this Element's sections, but can also integrate the social interpretation of the four theatrical processes into its performances. As demonstrated in the discussion of *Ghosts*, performing the processes where they are not overtly signalled can offer new political perspectives. That is, while society may seek to

---

[169] Bert O. States, *Great Reckonings in Little Rooms. On the Phenomenology of Theater* (Berkeley: University of California Press, 1985), p. 8.

[170] Dan Rebellato, 'When We Talk of Horses: Or, What Do We See When We See a Play?', *Performance Research*, 14: 1 (2009), pp. 17–28 (18).

portray itself as unchangeable, basing this on non-negotiable concepts such as sovereign individuality, fixed identity, authenticity or the inevitability of social systems, theatre can show how it does this. And when the mechanisms have been exposed, human beings gain the means to change them. Such change is, of course, difficult and takes time, but even a suggestion of change can refashion spectators' consciousness.

Theatricality can no longer be considered an area of particular interest in Theatre Studies. It not only pervades theatrical performance and the playtext, it also unavoidably structures everyday social relations. That theatricality has often been understood as a special kind of behaviour or practice, detectable only through ostentation or overt signalling, is no longer tenable. Instead, we can start to investigate playtexts for the function of both overt and covert theatricality and develop approaches to performance that necessarily, ostentatiously, allow the interdependent processes to resonate on stage. Performance can politicize theatricality in order to reveal ways that society seeks to deny theatricality in everyday life and to contemplate societies in which the four theatrical processes are recognized and refunctioned, following the analysis of *Ghosts*, in the interest of a fairer, more egalitarian world.

Bibliography

Primary Sources

Aeschylus, *The Eumenides*, in Aeschylus, *The Oresteia: Agamemnon, the Libation Bearers, the Eumenides*, Robert Fagles (trans.) (London: Penguin, 1977), pp. 225–77.

Beckett, Samuel, *Catastrophe*, in Beckett (ed.), *The Complete Dramatic Works* (London: Faber & Faber, 1986), pp. 455–61.

Brecht, Bertolt, 'Can the Present-Day World Be Reproduced by Means of Theatre?', in Marc Silberman, Steve Giles and Tom Kuhn (eds.), *Brecht on Theatre*, 3rd ed., (London: Bloomsbury, 2014), pp. 311–12.

Brecht, Bertolt, 'The Decision', John Willett (trans.), in John Willett (ed.), *Collected Plays*, Volume 3, (London: Bloomsbury, 1997), pp. 61–89.

Brecht, Bertolt, '[Plagiat und Kunst]', in Brecht, *Große kommentierte Berliner und Frankfurter Ausgabe*, Werner Hecht, Jan Knopf, Werner Mittenzwei and Klaus-Detlef Müller (eds.), Vol. 21 (Berlin: Aufbau, 1992), p. 318.

Brecht, Bertolt, 'Short Description of a New Technique of Acting That Produces a *Verfremdung* Effect', in Brecht, *Brecht on Theatre*, 3rd ed., Marc Silberman, Steve Giles and Tom Kuhn (eds.) (London: Bloomsbury, 2014), pp. 184–96.

Brecht, Bertolt, 'The Street Scene', in Brecht, *Brecht on Theatre*, 3rd ed., Marc Silberman, Steve Giles and Tom Kuhn (eds.) (London: Bloomsbury, 2014), pp. 176–83.

Churchill, Caryl, *Blue Kettle*, in Churchill, *Plays*, Volume 4 (London: Nick Hern, 2008), pp. 97–128.

Churchill, Caryl, *Heart's Desire*, in Churchill, *Plays*, Volume 4 (London: Nick Hern, 2008), pp. 63–95.

Churchill, Caryl, 'Introduction', in Churchill, *Plays*, Volume 4 (London: Nick Hern, 2008), pp. vii–x.

Jackie Sibblies Drury, *Fairview* (New York: Theatre Communications Group, 2019).

Handke, Peter, 'Introduction', Michael Roloff (trans.), in Handke (ed.), *Plays*, Volume 1 (London: Methuen, 1997), pp. 53–55.

Handke, Peter, *Kaspar*, Michael Roloff (trans.), in Handke (ed.), *Plays*, Volume 1 (London: Methuen, 1997), pp. 51–141.

Ibsen, Henrik, *Ghosts*, student edition, Non Worrall (ed.), Michael Meyer (trans.) (Bloomsbury: London, 2008).

Smith, Anna Deavere, 'Introduction', in Smith (ed.), *Fires in the Mirror: Crown Heights Brooklyn and Other Identities* (New York: Anchor, 1993), pp. xxiii–xli.

Smith, Anna Deavere, *Fires in the Mirror: Crown Heights Brooklyn and Other Identities* (New York: Anchor, 1993).

Secondary Sources

Abel, Lionel, *Tragedy and Metatheatre: Essays on Dramatic Form*, introduced by Martin Puchner (NY: Holmes and Meyer, 2003).

Adorno, Theodor, 'Commitment', in Theodor Adorno, Walter Benjamin, Ernst Bloch, Bertolt Brecht and Georg Lukács (eds.), *Aesthetics and Politics* (London: Verso, 2007), pp. 177–195.

Aston, Elaine, *Caryl Churchill*, 2nd ed. (Tavistock: Northcote House, 2001).

Barish, Jonas, *The Antitheatrical Prejudice* (Berkeley: University of California Press, 1981).

Barnett, David, 'When Is a Play Not a Drama? Two Examples of Postdramatic Theatre Texts', *New Theatre Quarterly*, 24: 1 (2008), pp. 14–23.

Barthes, Roland, 'Baudelaire's Theater', in Roland Barthes, *Critical Essays*, translated by Richard Howard (Evanston: Northwestern University Press, 1972), pp. 25–31.

Boenisch, Peter M., *Directing Scenes and Senses: The Thinking of 'Regie'* (Manchester: Manchester University Press, 2015).

Botelho, Teresa, 'The Dramatization of Cross-Identity Voicing and the Poetics of Ambiguity', *Hungarian Journal of English and American Studies*, 15: 1 (2009), pp. 79–97.

Brenner, Eva Elisabeth, *'Hamletmachine' Onstage: A Critical Analysis of Heiner Müller's Play in Production.* (PhD thesis, New York University, 1994).

Bromley, David W., *Possessive Individualism: A Crisis of Capitalism* (Oxford: Oxford University Press, 2019).

Burns, Elizabeth. *Theatricality: A Study of Convention in the Theatre and in Social Life* (New York: Harper & Row, 1972).

Butler, Judith, 'Performative Acts and Gender Constitution: An Essay in Phenomenology and Feminist Theory', *Theatre Journal*, 40:4 (1988), pp. 519–31.

Cascetta, Annamaria. *Modern European Tragedy: Exploring Crucial Plays* (London: Anthem, 2014).

Collini, Stefan, 'Defending Cultural Criticism', *New Left Review*, 18 (2002), pp. 73–97. https://newleftreview.org/issues/ii18/articles/stefan-collini-defending-cultural-criticism [accessed 29 August 2023].

Conze, Eckart, 'Eine bürgerliche Republik? Bürgertum und Bürgerlichkeit in der westdeutschen Nachkriegsgesellschaft', *Geschichte und Gesellschaft*, 30:3 (2004), pp. 527–42.

Derrida, Jacques, 'Differance', in Jacques Derrida (ed.), *Speech and Phenomena and Other Essays on Husserl's Theory of Signs*, tr. by David B. Allison (Evanston: Northwestern University Press, 1973) pp. 129–60.

DiAngelo, Robin, 'New Racism', *Counterpoints*, 398 (2012), pp. 105–32.

Dolan, Jill, '"Finding Our Feet in the Shoes of (One An) Other": Multiple Character Solo Performers and Utopian Performatives, *Modern Drama*, 45:4 (2002), pp. 495–18.

Donnellan, Declan, *The Actor and the Target* (London: Nick Hern, 2002).

Dugdale, Eric and Loramy Gerstbauerpolis, 'Forms of Justice in Aeschylus' *Eumenides*', *Polis*, 34 (2017), pp. 226–50.

Durbach, Errol, 'The Dramatic Poetry of Ibsen's Ghosts', *Mosaic*, 11:4 (1978), pp. 55–66.

Easterling, Pat, 'Theatrical Furies: Thoughts on *Eumenides*', in Martin Revermann and Peter Wilson (eds.), *Performance, Iconography, Reception: Studies in Honour of Oliver Taplin* (Oxford: Oxford University Press, 2008), pp. 219–36.

Edwards, Paul J., 'Catering to White Audiences: *Fairview* at Woolly Mammoth', *The Drama Review*, 65: 2 (2021), pp. 173–78.

Eggington, William. *How the World Became a Stage: Presence, Theatricality and the Question of Modernity* (Albany: State University of New York Press, 2003).

Feffer, Steve, 'Extending the Breaks: *Fires in the Mirror* in the Context of Hip-Hop Structure, Style, and Culture', *Comparative Drama*, 37: 3&4 (2003–04), pp. 397–415.

Féral, Josette, 'Theatricality: The Specificity of Theatrical Language', *SubStance*, 31: 2&3 (2002), pp. 94–108.

Ferran, Peter W., 'New Measures for Brecht in America', *Theater*, 25:2 (1994), pp. 9–23.

Fiebach, Joachim, 'Theatricality: From Oral Traditions to Televised "Realities"', *SubStance*, 31: 2&3 (2002), pp. 17–41.

Fischer-Lichte, Erika, 'Theatricality: A Key Concept in Theatre and Cultural Studies', *Theatre Research International*, 20:2 (1995), pp. 85–89.

Fischer-Lichte, Erika, 'Verwandlung als ästhetische Kategorie: Zur Entwicklung einer neuen Ästhetik des Performativen', in Fischer-Lichte, Friedemann Kreuder and Isabel Pflug (eds.), *Theater seit den 60er Jahren. Grenzgänge der Neo-Avantgarde* (Tübingen: A Franke, 1998), pp. 21–91.

Freshwater, Helen, *Theatre & Audience* (London: Methuen, 2009).

Friedrich, Rainer, 'Brecht and Postmodernism', *Philosophy and Literature*, 23: 1 (1999), pp. 44–64.

Frisina, Kyle C., 'Contemporary African-American Drama at Visuality's Limits', *Modern Drama*, 63:2 (2020), pp. 197–220.

Gadamer, Hans-Georg, *Truth and Method*, 2nd ed., tr. by Joel Weinsheimer and Donald G. Marshall (New York: Crossroad, 1989).

Gobert, R. Darren, 'On Performance and Selfhood in Caryl Churchill', in Elaine Aston and Elin Diamond (eds.), *The Cambridge Companion to Caryl Churchill* (Cambridge: Cambridge University Press, 2009), pp. 105–124.

Gobert, R. Darren, *The Theatre of Caryl Churchill* (London: Bloomsbury, 2014).

Goffman, Irving, *The Presentation of Self in Everyday Life* (London: Penguin, 1969).

Hall, Edith, 'Peaceful Conflict Resolution and Its Discontents in Aeschylus's *Eumenides*', *Common Knowledge*, 21: 2 (2015), pp. 253–69.

Hancock, Ange-Marie, *Intersectionality: An Intellectual History* (New York: Oxford University Press, 2016).

Hansen, Jim, 'Samuel Beckett's *Catastrophe* and the Theater of Pure Means', *Contemporary Literature*, 49:4 (2008), pp. 660–82.

Heim, Caroline, *Audience as Performer: The Changing Role of Theatre Audiences in the Twenty-First Century* (London: Routledge, 2016).

Hilfrich, Carola, 'Aesthetics of Unease: A Brechtian Study of Anna Deavere Smith's Eyewitness Performance in *Fires in the Mirror*', *Partial Answers*, 7: 2 (2009), pp. 299–318.

Hill, Linda, 'Obscurantism and Verbal Resistance in Handke's *Kaspar*', *The Germanic Review*, 52:4 (1977), pp. 304–15.

Hornby, Richard, *Drama, Metadrama, and Perception* (London: Associated Universities Presses, 1986).

Jay, Gregory, 'Other People's Holocausts: Trauma, Empathy, and Justice in Anna Deavere Smith's *Fires in the Mirror*', *Contemporary Literature*, 48: 1 (2007), pp. 119–50.

Jernigan, Daniel, '*Traps, Softcops, Blue Heart*, and *This Is a Chair*: Tracking Epistemological Upheaval in Caryl Churchill's Shorter Plays', *Modern Drama*, 47: 1 (2004), pp. 21–43.

Kalb, Jonathan, *Beckett in Performance* (Cambridge: Cambridge University Press, 1989).

Knapp, Bettina L., 'Peter Handke's *Kaspar*: The Mechanics of Language – A Fractionating Schizophrenic Theatrical Event', *Studies in 20th Century Literature*, 14:2 (1990), pp. 241–59.

Krometis, Damon, 'Sitting on the Couch: The Conundrum of Spectatorship in Jackie Sibblies Drury's *Fairview*', *Journal of Dramatic Theory and Criticism*, 37:1 (2022), pp. 67–86.

Komins, Benton Jay, 'Rewriting, Violence, and Theater: Bertolt Brecht's *The Measures Taken* and Heiner Müller's *Mauser*', *The Comparatist*, 26 (2002), pp. 99–119.

Kotte, Andreas, *Studying Theatre: Phenomena, Structures and Functions* (Vienna: Lit Verlag, 2010).

Kumar, Vaibhav, and M. L. Garg, 'Predictive Analytics: A Review of Trends and Techniques', *International Journal of Computer Applications*, 182:1 (2018), pp. 31–37.

Landy, Robert J., *Persona and Performance: The Meaning of Role in Drama, Therapy, and Everyday Life* (London: Jessica Kingsley, 1993).

Lehmann, Hans-Thies, *Postdramatic Theatre*, translated by Karen Jürs-Munby (Abingdon: Routledge, 2006).

Libera, Antoni, 'Beckett's *Catastrophe*', *Modern Drama*, 28: 3 (1985), pp. 341–47.

Maxwell, Ian, 'Teaching Performance Studies with Brecht's *Lehrstück* Model: *The Measures Taken*', *Brecht Yearbook*, 41 (2019), pp. 76–97.

McDonald, Marianne, *The Living Art of Greek Tragedy* (Bloomington: Indiana University Press, 2003).

McMullan, Anna, *Theatre on Trial: Samuel Beckett's Later Drama* (London: Routledge, 1993).

McTighe, Trish, 'Everyday Catastrophes: Gender, Labour and Power in Beckett's Theatre. Structural Maintenance', *Journal of Beckett Studies*, 28:1 (2019), pp. 19–34.

Merlin, Bella, 'Acting Hare: *The Permanent Way*', in Richard Boon (ed.), *The Cambridge Companion to David Hare* (Cambridge: Cambridge University Press, 2007), pp. 123–37.

Moorjani, Angela, 'Directing or In-Directing Beckett: Or What Is Wrong with *Catastrophe*'s Director?', S*amuel Beckett Today*, 15 (2005), pp. 187–99.

Nellhaus, Tobin, 'Online Role-Playing Games and the Definition of Theatre', *New Theatre Quarterly*, 33:4 (2017), pp. 345–359.

Nelson, Robert J., *Play within a Play: The Dramatist's Conception of His Art: Shakespeare to Anouilh* (New Haven: Yale University Press, 1958).

Newton, K. M., *Modern Literature and the Tragic* (Edinburgh: Edinburgh University Press, 2008).

Olsson, Ulf, *Silence and Subject in Modern Literature: Spoken Violence* (Basingstoke: Palgrave, 2013).

Pearce, Michael, 'Making Whiteness Visible and Felt in *Fairview*', *Humanities*, 10:2 (2021), pp. 1–16.

Peja, Laura, 'Victimized Actors and Despotic Directors: Cliches of Theatre at Stake in Beckett's *Catastrophe*', in S. E. Gontarski (ed.), *The Edinburgh Companion to Samuel Beckett and the Arts* (Edinburgh: Edinburgh University Press, 2014), pp. 386–96.

Postlewait, Thomas and Tracy C. Davis, 'Theatricality: An Introduction', in Davis and Postlewait (eds.), *Theatricality* (Cambridge: Cambridge University Press, 2003), pp. 1–39.

Puchner, Martin, 'Introduction', in Lionel Abel (ed.), *Tragedy and Metatheatre: Essays on Dramatic Form*, introduced by Martin Puchner (NY: Holmes and Meyer, 2003), pp. 1–24.

Puchner, Martin, *Stage Fright: Modernism, Anti-Theatricality & Drama* (Baltimore: Johns Hopkins University Press, 2002).

Rabascall, Enric Monforte, *Gender, Politics, Subjectivity: Reading Caryl Churchill* (unpublished doctoral thesis, University of Barcelona, 2000).

Read, M., 'Peter Handke's *Kaspar* and the Power of Negative Thinking', *Forum for Modern Language Studies*, 24:2 (1993), pp. 126–48.

Realo, Anu, Kati Koido, Eva Ceulemans and Jüri Allik, 'Three Components of Individualism', *European Journal of Personality*, 16: 3 (2002), pp. 163–84.

Rebellato, Dan, 'When We Talk of Horses: Or, What Do We See When We See a Play?', *Performance Research*, 14: 1 (2009), pp. 17–28.

Reinelt, Janelle, 'Performing Race: Anna Deavere Smith's *Fires in the Mirror*', *Modern Drama*, 39 (1996), pp. 609–17.

Reinelt, Janelle, 'The Politics of Discourse: Performativity Meets Theatricality', *SubStance*, 31: 2&3 (2002), pp. 201–15.

Rekdal, Anne Marie, 'The Freedom of Perversion: A Lacanian Reading of Ibsen's *Ghosts*', *Ibsen Studies*, 5: 2 (2005), pp. 121–47.

Ringer, Mark, *Electra, and the Empty Urn: Metatheater and Role Playing in Sophocles* (Chapel Hill: University of North Carolina Press, 1998).

Roth, Andrew, '"Don't call it a war" – Propaganda filters the truth about Ukraine on Russian media', *The Guardian*, 26 February 2022.

Sauter, Willmar, *The Theatrical Event: Dynamics of Performance and Perception* (Iowa: University of Iowa Press, 2000).

Schechner, Richard, 'Anna Deavere Smith: Acting as Incorporation', *The Drama Review*, 37:4 (1993), pp. 63–64.

Schechner, Richard, *Performance Theory*, revised and expanded edition (London: Routledge, 2003).

Schlueter, June, '"Goats and Monkeys" and the "Idiocy of Language": Handke's *Kaspar* and Shakespeare's *Othello*', *Modern Drama*, 23:1 (1980), pp. 25–32.

Sedgman, Kirsty, 'Audience Experience in an Anti-Expert Age: A Survey of Theatre Audience Research', *Theatre Research International*, 42: 3 (2018), pp. 307–22.

Sheppard, Richard, *Tankred Dorst's 'Toller': A Case Study in Reception* (New Alyth: Lochee, 1989).

Simons, Oliver, 'Theater of Revolution and the Law of Genre: Bertolt Brecht's *The Measures Taken* (*Die Maßnahme*)', *The Germanic Review*, 84: 4 (2009), pp. 327–52.

Sprinchorn, Evert, 'Syphilis in Ibsen's *Ghosts*', *Ibsen Studies*, 4:2 (2004), pp. 191–204.

States, Bert O., '*Catastrophe*: Beckett's Laboratory/Theatre', *Modern Drama*, 30: 1 (1987), pp. 14–22.

States, Bert O., *Great Reckonings in Little Rooms: On the Phenomenology of Theater* (Berkeley: University of California Press, 1985).

Stegemann, Bernd, *Lob des Realismus* (Berlin: Theater der Zeit, 2015).

Stein, Juana Christina von, 'The Theater of the Absurd and the Absurdity of Theater: The Early Plays of Beckett and Ionesco', in Elena Penskaya and Joachim Küpper (eds.), *Theater as Metaphor* (Berlin: De Gruyter, 2019), pp. 217-237.

Steinberger, Peter J., 'Eumenides and the Invention of Politics', *Polis*, 39 (2022), pp. 77–98.

Stockhammer, Robert, 'We Shall Therefore Never Write about What Took Place or Did Not Take Place in May', *Interventions*, 23:3 (2021), pp. 448–62.

Sun, William H. and Faye C. Fei, 'Masks or Faces Revisited: A Study of Four Theatrical Works Concerning Cultural Identity', *The Drama Review*, 38: 4 (1994), pp. 120–32.

Thompson, Debby, '"Is Race a Trope?": Anna Deavere Smith and the Question of Racial Performativity', *African American Review*, 37: 1 (2003), pp. 127–38.

Watten, Barrett, 'The Bride of the Assembly Line: Radical Poetics in Construction', in Maria Damon and Ira Livingston (eds.), *Poetry and Cultural Studies: A Reader* (Chicago: University of Illinois Press, 2009) pp. 163–76.

Weber, Carl, 'Brecht's "Street Scene" – On Broadway of All Places? A Conversation with Anna Deavere Smith', *Brecht Yearbook*, 20 (1995), pp. 51–63.

Weber, Samuel, *Theatricality as Medium* (New York: Fordham University Press, 2004).

Wilshire, Bruce, *Role Playing and Identity: The Limits of Theatre as Metaphor* (Bloomington: Indiana University Press, 1982).

Wolterman, Nick, 'Playing the Crowd: Beckett, Havel, and Their Audiences', *Textual Practice*, 34:4 (2020), pp. 691–712.

Zola, Émile, 'Naturalism on the Stage', in Toby Cole (ed.), *Playwrights on Playwriting: From Ibsen to Ionesco* (New York: Cooper Square Press, 2001), pp. 5–14.

Acknowledgements

I would like to thank the series' editorial team, Fintan Walsh, Duška Radosavljević and Caridad Svich, for their lightning-fast acceptance of my book proposal and their collective encouragement. I am also grateful to the two anonymous peer reviewers, particularly to the one who suggested a far superior articulation of my third theatrical process. Emily Hockley at Cambridge University Press has also helped greatly. And I am indebted, metaphorically thank goodness, to the University of York for funding the not inconsiderable fee that has made this Element available to all through open access.

About the Author

David Barnett is Professor of Theatre at the University of York. He has authored monographs on Heiner Müller (Routledge, 2016; Peter Lang, 1998), The Berliner Ensemble (Cambridge University Press, 2015), Brecht's theatre practice (Bloomsbury, 2014), and Fassbinder's theatre (Cambridge University Press, 2005). He has written several articles and essays on political and postdramatic theatre.

Cambridge Elements ☰

Contemporary Performance Texts

Senior Editor
Fintan Walsh
Birkbeck, University of London

Fintan Walsh is a Professor of Performing Arts and Humanities at Birkbeck, University of London. He is the Head of the School of Creative Arts, Culture, and Communication and the Director of Birkbeck Centre for Contemporary Theatre. He is also a former Senior Editor of *Theatre Research International.*

Associate Editors
Duska Radosavljevic
Royal Central School of Speech and Drama, University of London.

Duška Radosavljević is a Professorial Research Fellow at the Royal Central School of Speech and Drama. Her work has received the David Bradby Research Prize (2015), the Elliott Hayes Award for Dramaturgy (2022), and the ATHE-ASTR Award for Digital Scholarship.

Caridad Svich
Rutgers University

Caridad Svich is a playwright and translator. She teaches creative writing and playwriting in the English Department at Rutgers University-New Brunswick.

Advisory Board
Siân Adiseshiah, *Loughborough University*
Helena Grehan, *Murdoch University*
Ameet Parameswaran, *Jawaharlal Nehru University*
Synne Behrndt, *Stockholm University of the Arts*
Jay Pather, *University of Cape Town*
Sodja Zupanc Lotker, *The Academy of Performing Arts in Prague (DAMU).*
Peter M. Boenisch, *Aarhus University*
Hayato Kosuge, *Keio University*
Edward Ziter, *NYU Tisch School of the Arts*
Milena Gras Kleiner, *Pontificia Universidad Católica de Chile*
Savas Patsalidis, *Aristotle University, Thessaloniki, Greece*
Harvey Young, *College of Fine Arts, Boston University*

About the Series
Contemporary Performance Texts responds to the evolution of the form, role and meaning of text in theatre and performance in the late twentieth and twenty-first centuries, by publishing Elements that explore the generation of text for performance, its uses in performance, and its varied modes of reception and documentation.

Cambridge Elements ≡

Contemporary Performance Texts

Elements in the Series

Milton Keynes UK
Ingram Content Group UK Ltd.
UKHW020842270524
443303UK00007B/30

9 781009 506298